FUN IN PARIS

New titles in the series

Las Vegas
New York City
Orlando Area

also available

Acapulco
Bahamas
London
Montreal
Puerto Rico
San Francisco
St. Martin/Sint Maarten
Waikiki

FODOR'S

FUN IN PARIS

1988

Paul Ross

FODOR'S TRAVEL PUBLICATIONS, INC.
New York & London

Copyright © 1987 by Fodor's Travel Publications, Inc.

All rights reserved under International and Pan-American Copyright Conventions. Published in the United States by Fodor's Travel Publications, Inc., and subsidiary of Random House, Inc., New York, and simultaneously in Canada by Random House of Canada Limited, Toronto. Distributed by Random House, Inc., New York.

ISBN 0-679-01513-2
ISBN 0-340-41965-2 (Hodder and Stoughton edition)

Maps and plans by Swanston Graphics
Illustrations by Ted Burwell

MANUFACTURED IN THE UNITED STATES OF AMERICA
10 9 8 7 6 5 4 3 2 1

Contents

Map of Paris, viii–ix

Paris Briefing *Map of Paris Métro,* 8–9	1
Introducing Paris *Map of Paris Arrondissements,* 13	12
The Eiffel Tower and Champs Elysées *Map of the Champs Elysées,* 20	18
The Tuileries and the Louvre *Map of the Louvre,* 28	24
Around the Opéra *Map of the Opéra Area,* 30	29
Montmartre *Map of Montmartre,* 39	38
The Beaubourg and the Marais *Map of the Marais,* 46	43
The Ile St.-Louis and Ile de la Cité *Map of the Ile de la Cité,* 50	49
The Left Bank *Map of the Left Bank,* 56–57	54

CONTENTS *vi*

Hotels	63
Restaurants	71
Cafés and Bars	84
Nightlife	89
Music, Movies, and Theaters	94
Shopping	101
Index	111

Map of Paris

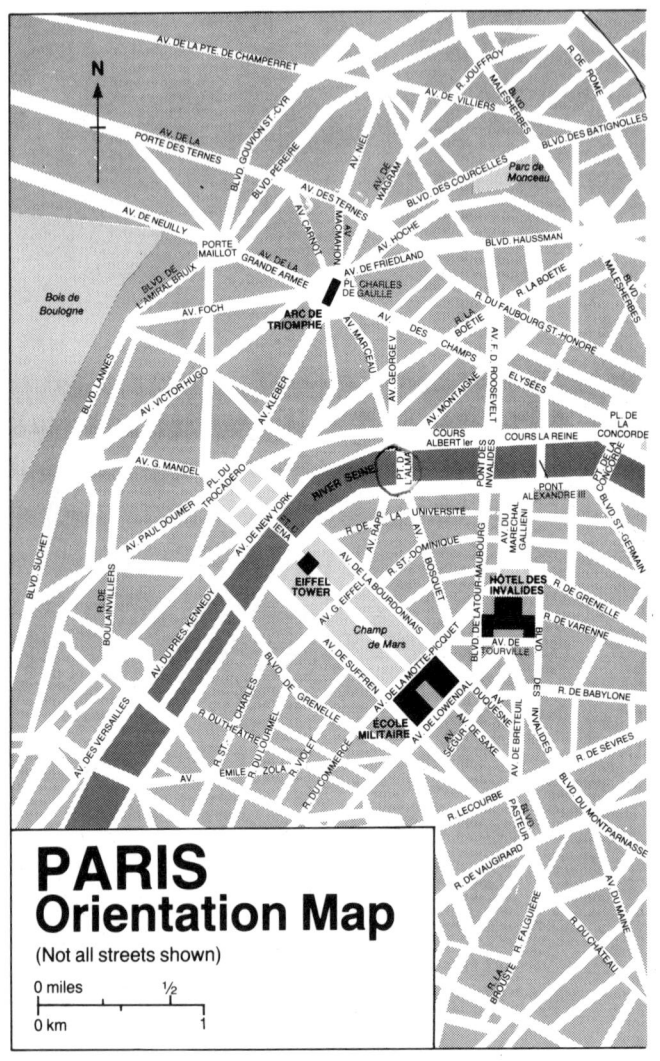

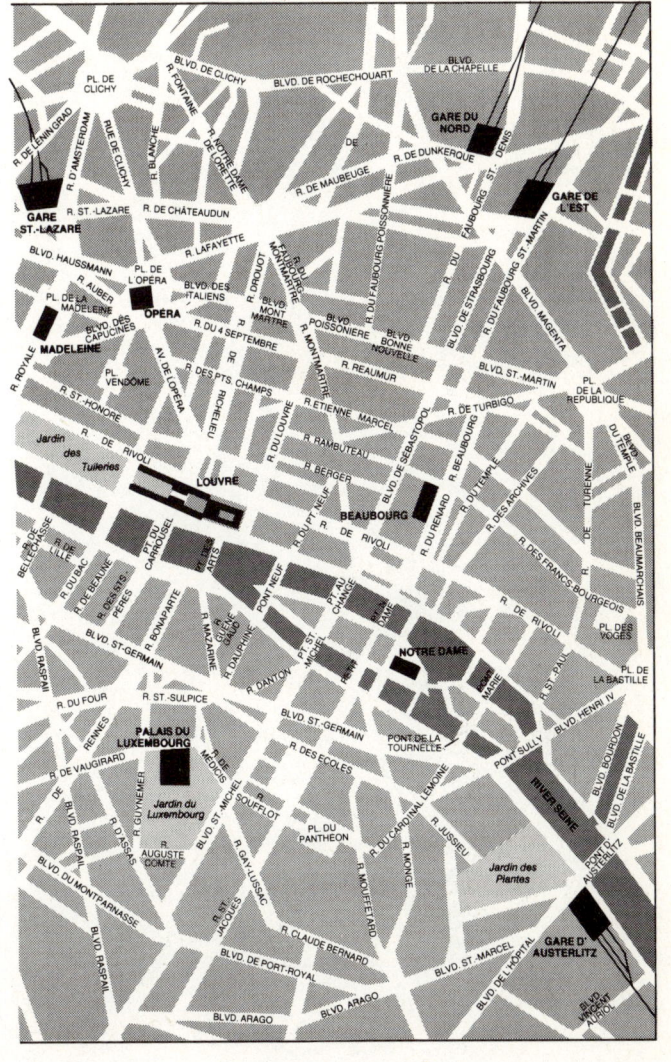

Paris Briefing

Make the French National Tourist Office the first stop on your visit to Paris. They have offices throughout the globe and can supply a wealth of information on the French capital, much of it free and all of it useful. Their principal offices are:

● **In the U.S.:** 610 Fifth Avenue, New York, NY 10020 (tel. 212–757–1125); 645 North Michigan Avenue, Chicago, IL 60611 (tel. 312–337–6301); 1 Hallidie, Suite 250, San Francisco, CA 94182 (tel. 415–986–4161); 9401 Wilshire Boulevard, Suite 314, Beverly Hills, CA 90212 (tel. 213–272–2661).

● **In Canada:** 1981 Avenue McGill College, Montreal, Quebec H3A 2W9 (tel. 514–288–4264); 1 Dundas Street West, Suite 2405, Box 8, Toronto, Ontario M5G 1Z3 (tel. 416–593–4717).

● **In the U.K.:** 178 Piccadilly, London W1V OAL (tel. 01–491–7622).

You'll be equally well catered for in Paris itself. The main Paris Tourist Office is at 127 avenue des Champs-Elysées, 75008 Paris (tel. 47-23-61-72). Open 9 A.M. to 10 P.M. Monday to Saturday in summer, 9 A.M. to 8 P.M.

Sunday and public holidays in summer and every day in winter. The office is crammed with information on Paris and can also supply brochures for other parts of the country if you're traveling on. The multilingual hostesses can make hotel reservations for a small charge (not more than five days in advance) and in the same building you'll find the main office of the S.N.C.F. (French Rail) tourist office.

There is a special recorded-message telephone information service for details of the week's events—concerts, ballet, exhibits, parades, son-et-lumière, special events of all kinds. Called *Sélection Losisirs*, it offers a version in English, reached by dialing 47-20-88-98 (though you may need to listen to it twice round, as the pronunciation sometimes leaves a lot to be desired).

There is also a tourist information office in the Mairie or City Hall (just by Hôtel-de-Ville métro stop). And the City of Paris puts up posters all over the city giving details of one-time events—parades, firework displays, and the like. You name it, they organize it.

There are branch offices at Est, Lyon, and Nord rail stations; and at the Palais des Congrès at the Porte Maillot, but these may be closed Sundays and public holidays.

• **What's On.** Information on what's on in Paris during your stay is best gleaned from the weekly *L'Officiel des Spectacles* or the slightly more expensive *Pariscope*, both available from all newsstands and drugstores, and full of information. Both appear on Wednesday, the day the movie programs change. Your hotel will probably have a copy of the free weekly *Paris-Sélection*, which is also obtainable from some travel agencies and tourist offices.

The national dailies *Le Figaro, Le Monde, Libération, La Croix*, and *France-Soir* give full details of movies, theaters, opera and ballet, exhibits, and other events. Other useful sources are the *International Herald Tribune*, published daily in Paris, and the English-language fortnightly *Passion*.

Over 50 of Paris's top hotels have installed an electronic information system known as *Cititel*. This will provide answers to a huge range of questions about cultural events in Paris and the whole of the Ile de France region.

MONEY MATTERS

Safeguard yourself by taking traveler's checks; be sure to note the serial numbers separately. But get some francs before you leave. The airport banks will be open whatever time you arrive, but there are usually long lines, and the rates aren't all that great anyway. Paris's banks are open from 9 to 4:30, Monday to Friday, though some close from 12 to 2. They all close on the day before a public holiday. Central Paris has a number of *bureaux de change,* many open late, but they will invariably give lower rates than a bank. Similarly, you can change money at hotels, some stores, and even the odd restaurant, but again you'll get a poor rate. You can also change money in post offices (*bureaux de poste*) which are open 9 to 7, Monday to Friday, and 9 to 12 on Saturday. Rates are similar to those given by the banks.

The major credit cards are accepted in most of the better hotels, restaurants and shops, but check the doors and windows for the usual stickers carefully. Many thrifty Parisian proprietors are damned if they see why they should pay over their hard-earned cash in a percentage to the credit card companies, and refuse to take *any* kind of card.

CLIMATE

Variable, as in most northern European countries. Summer can be hot, and most Parisians sensibly leave Paris to the tourists in August. Fall can be warm and mellow, and winter very cold with snow but also with beautifully clear, crisp days (on the other hand it can also be just plain awful). Spring brings contrasting spells of overcast skies with rain, and the clear blue skies which inspired the song *April in Paris*.

Clothes

The French are nothing if not fashion conscious. Parisian chic is visible everywhere: in the street, restaurants, the opera, the métro. Choose clothes to fit the occasion, to feel comfortable whether you're going to a Gala night at the Opéra or spending the day sightseeing. But leave space in your case for anything you buy. And take an umbrella or raincoat and a pair of sunglasses.

Time

France is six hours ahead of Eastern Standard Time and one hour ahead of Greenwich Mean Time. The French put their clocks forward an hour in the spring and back an hour in the fall at more or less the same time as both the U.S. and Britain.

Entry and customs

All foreign nationals must have a valid passport to enter France. *All* visitors from outside the Common Market countries, including Americans and Canadians, must also have a visa.

There are two levels of duty-free allowance for travelers entering France: one, for those coming from an E.E.C. country; two, for those coming from any other country.
- In the first category you may import duty free: 1) 300 cigarettes, 150 cigarillos, 75 cigars, 400 gr. of tobacco; 2)

three liters of wine and one and a half liters of alcohol over 22° proof, or three liters of alcohol less than 22° proof; 3) 75 gr. of perfume and three-eighths of a liter of toilet water; 4) for those over 15, other goods to the value of 2,000 frs. (400 frs. for those under 15).

• In the second category you may import duty free: 1) 200 cigarettes, 100 cigarillos, 50 cigars, or 250 gr. of tobacco (these allowances are doubled if you live outside Europe); 2) two liters of wine, and two liters of alcohol less than 22° proof, or one liter of alcohol more than 22° proof; 3) 50 gr. of perfume and a quarter of a liter of toilet water; 4) for those over 15, other goods to the value of 300 frs. (150 frs. for those under 15).

Any amount of French or foreign currency may be imported into France. Foreign currencies converted into francs may be reconverted into foreign currency only up to the equivalent of 5,000 frs. Similarly, no more than 5,000 frs. may be exported. No more than the equivalent of 2,000 frs. in foreign currency may be exported.

Tipping

Hotels, restaurants, and cafés will always automatically include the service charge in your check, so don't tip unless you think it's really justified, in which case 12 to 15 per cent is about normal. Otherwise, tip as you would back home.

Getting around

• **From the Airports:** Getting into town from both the city's main airports—Roissy/Charles de Gaulle, the major airport, and Orly—is easy. There are buses from both every 15 minutes between 5.30 A.M. and 11 P.M. Buses from Roissy go to the Porte Maillot terminal in the northwest of the city, from Orly to Les Invalides terminal on the Left Bank. Journey times are around 30 to 40 minutes depending on the traffic.

There are trains to the Gare du Nord from Roissy, and the Gare d'Austerlitz and the Gare St.-Michel from Orly. Trains leave every 15 minutes, and the trip takes about 30 minutes. All the airport trains link up with the R.E.R. express métro system, meaning that you can easily change onto the regular métro.

Taxis are plentiful at both airports and will take you into the center of Paris for around 180 frs., including tip.

- **City Transportation:** Modern Paris is a bustling, noisy city, full of traffic and very impatient drivers who hoot at everything that moves and who will park sideways up a wall if given a chance. You'll need the agility of a cat to avoid these two- and four-wheeled menaces. They are no respecters of pedestrians—especially if they're clutching guidebooks.

Having said which, the public transport system in Paris is excellent, *if* you can avoid the rush hours. The best way to get around is on the métro; it's fast, efficient, and clean. There are maps in every station, some of which will light up your route at the touch of a button. Look for the name of the station at the end of the line you take. For example, if you are traveling from the Gare du Nord to St.-Germain-des-Pres, you take the line marked "Direction Porte d'Orléans."

There are both first-and second-class cars, but, whichever you use, buy a *carnet*, a little book of ten tickets —29 frs. for second class, 42 frs. for first. They're less expensive than regular tickets and eliminate the need to wait in line. You can buy them at all stations, as well as on buses, tobacco counters, and any other shop showing the R.A.T.P. sign, the Paris transport authority. All tickets can be used on buses and the métro. If you're traveling outside the central zone, simply add more tickets; otherwise, all trips are flat rate. Métro tickets are also good for the funicular railway up to Sacré-Coeur. Remember to keep your ticket with you after you've punched it into the automatic machine or you may be fined.

An excellent travel bargain is the Paris Sésame pass, giving unlimited travel on all métro and R.E.R. trains and

7 PARIS BRIEFING

buses. It's valid for two, for four or seven days, and is available from Roissy/Charles de Gaulle and Orly airports; the Paris tourist office; the head office of the R.A.T.P. (53 bis quai des Grands Augustins, 6e); and around 50 métro stations. Take your passport with you when you buy it.

The bus network is good, even if journey times are longer than on the métro. But it's a good way of seeing the city, and as each bus has a map of its route inside, with every stop marked, you needn't worry about missing your stop. Ring the bell to ask the driver to stop if the red *Arrêt demandé* sign isn't already lit up.

Taxis are a problem in Paris, mainly because there aren't enough of them. In theory you can hail them in the street if their lights are on, but many are reluctant to stop. The best plan is either to ask your hotel to call one for you, or to make for one of the city's numerous taxi ranks, *tête de ligne*, easily identified by the blue-and-white TAXI sign. Very few cabs will take more than three passengers. Any cab without a meter should be viewed with suspicion. If you *do* take one, agree on the fare before you set off.

● **Excursions and Detours.** There are numerous city bus tours taking in all the main sights with commentaries in every language from Serbo-Croat to Eskimo. The place des Pyramides at the east end of the Tuileries is where most set off from. Best-known and most reliable companies are: *American Express,* 11 rue Scribe, 9e (tel. 42-66-09-99); *Cityrama,* 4 pl. des Pyramides, 1er (tel. 42-60-30-14); *Paris Vision,* 214 rue de Rivoli, 1er (tel. 42-60-31-25).

For a more personal touch try *Hans Forster's Limousine Guide Service,* 202 rue de Rivoli, 1er (tel. 42-96-40-02). They can take up to seven passengers round the city and the surrounding areas for a minimum of three hours at $25 an hour. Reservations are essential.

Though sometimes crowded, a boat trip along the Seine is a marvelous way of seeing the city. There are a number of companies offering trips. Try: *Bateaux Mouches* (tel. 42-25-96-10), tours from the Pont de l'Alma, 8e, including evening trips with dinner (for which no children under 12 are allowed and "respectable" dress is

FUN IN PARIS 8

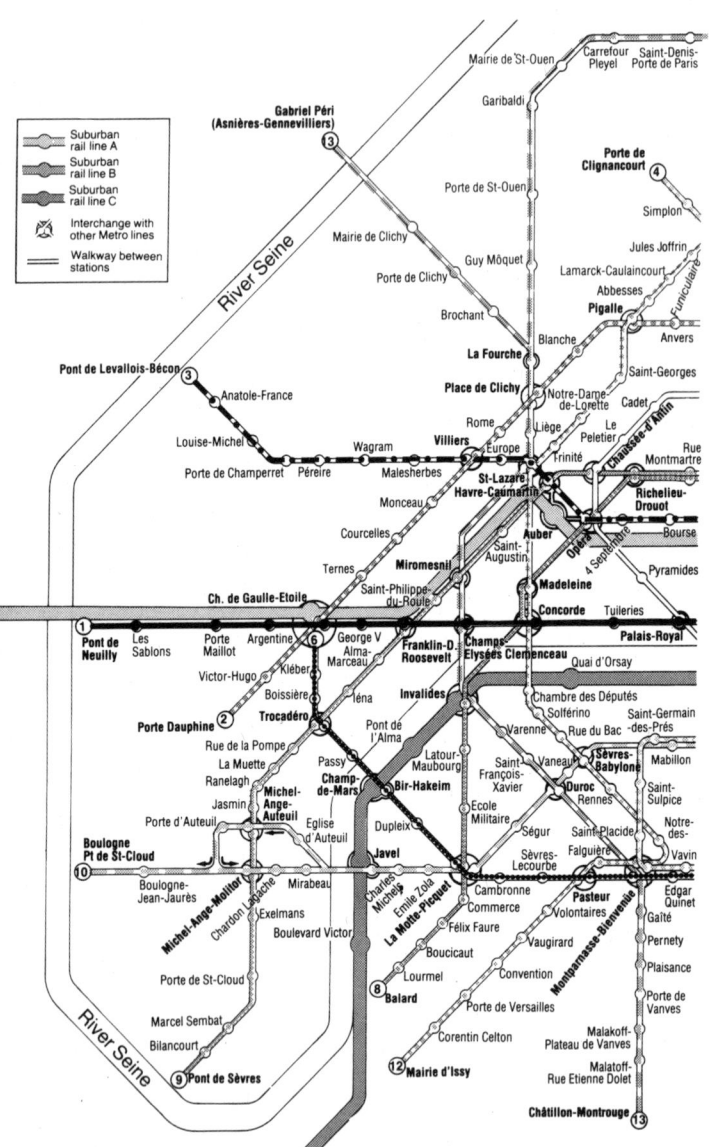

9 PARIS BRIEFING

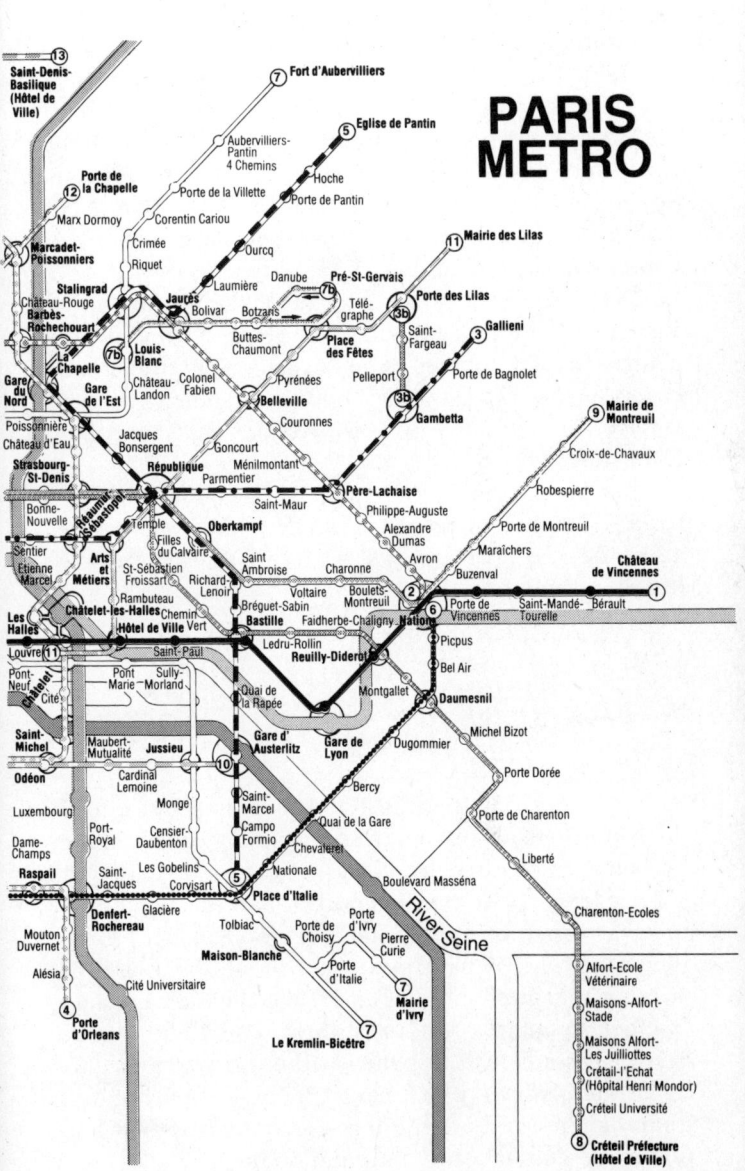

encouraged); *Bateaux Parisiens-Tour Eiffel* (tel. 45-51-33-08), tours from the south end of the Pont d'Iéna, again including evening trips with dinner on Friday and Saturday: *Vedettes Paris Ile-de-France* (tel. 47-05-71-29/45-50-23-79), tours from the Port de Suffren; *Vedettes du Pont Neuf* (tel. 46-33-93-38/43-29-86-19), tours from the Square du Vert Galant in the middle of the Pont Neuf.

Perhaps the ultimate tour around Paris is in a helicopter. *Hélicap* (tel. 45-57-75-51) have trips over Paris or La Défense on the western edge of the city or out to Versailles. Alternatively, they will devise a route of your choice, though obviously the farther you go the more it costs. *Chainair* (tel. 43-59-20-20) offer much the same service, but will also fly you over the châteaux of the Loire.

Back on terra firma again, bicycles can be rented from a number of places. Try: *La Maison du Vélo* (tel. 42-81-24-72); *Velocation* (tel. 43-54-67-21); or *Paris-Vélo* (tel. 43-37-59-22).

Tax refunds

Visitors to France (i.e. those normally resident outside the country) may be given the opportunity to save money by being exonerated from part of the value-added tax (*t.v.a.* in French) on certain goods. Discounts obtained in this way range from 13% to 23% (on "luxury" goods such as jewelry or perfumes). You should be aware that offering this discount is not a legal obligation on shopkeepers, so you may not insist on it. You'll find that the best places at which to benefit from the system are the department stores, which have special staff dealing with it, and shops with a large foreign clientele. Small boutiques are emphatically not equipped to deal efficiently with the complicated paperwork involved, and the system is liable to break down.

This is how it works. For a start, the total value of your purchases in a single store must be at least 1,200 frs. if you live outside the E.E.C.; if you live in an E.E.C. member state (which of course includes Britain and Ireland), discounts are obtainable only on *single items* costing at least 2,500 frs. Some stores will simply state a price after deduction of the discount. But they'll be taking a risk, because if you don't do your bit by handing on the documentation to customs, they'll be out of pocket. The great majority will ask you to pay the full amount and the discount will be sent to you in due course. The store will fill out a form in quadruplicate, giving you three copies and keeping one. Make sure that if you live outside the E.E.C. the store hasn't filled in an E.E.C. form by mistake and vice versa. You must give details of your bank account, or that of friends in France—reimbursements cannot be made to private addresses. If you live outside the E.E.C. you present two of the forms to the customs official on leaving the country—he will probably ask to see the goods in question to make sure that you haven't just been doing a favor to a French friend! Make sure to leave plenty of time for this operation. If you live in an E.E.C. country, the papers are dealt with by the customs official when you reach your own country.

Frankly, you may well think it's not worth the time and trouble, unless you're making really big purchases. And E.E.C.. residents in particular should bear in mind that the customs official you present your forms to back home may decide to charge you customs duty on the goods—which will easily cancel out the V.A.T. refund!

Introducing Paris

Paris, according to Henry James, is "an immense, amazing spectacle . . . a very good place to spend a fortune . . . a very good place for idle people." Or, as Victor Hugo put it, "To err is human. To loaf is Parisian."

Paris is a city of wonderful contrasts, from the vast, gilded salons of Proust's world on the boulevard Haussmann and the avenue de Messine, to the cramped, gray houses of the Left Bank, swamped in an air of desolate yet venerable grandeur and faded pomp, where old gardens lie between the gloomy, high walls. There are the Grands Boulevards, where shop windows display opulent wares, stunning fashions, and jewelry; there are crammed bookshops in narrow streets winding down to the *bouquiniste* stalls along the Seine; there are tiny shops hidden to the left and right of the rue St.-Denis and the rue St.-Martin, stuffed with bric-à-brac, not 500 yards from the gaudy lights of peep-shows, strip-clubs, and the low life of the once splendid district of Les Halles, Zola's fabled "belly of Paris," today home to the huge, modern Forum shopping mall.

There are magnificent walks to take and unforgettable sights to see: the imposing setting and perfect

13 INTRODUCING PARIS

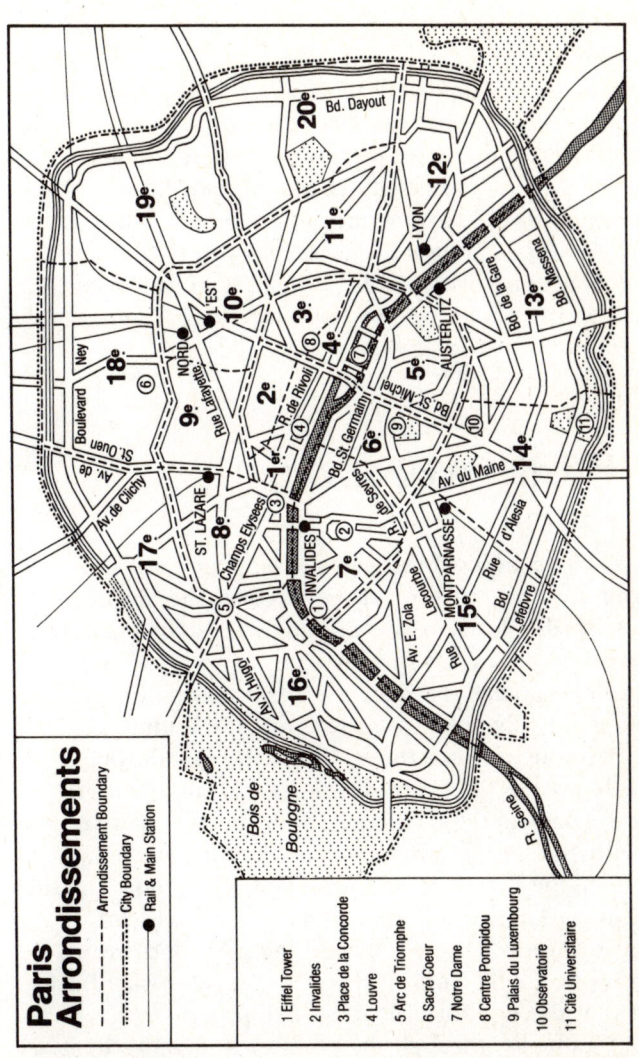

symmetry of the obelisk in the place de la Concorde; the grandiose views through the Tuileries from the Louvre stretching away to the west and, continuing the architectural line, straight up the Champs Elysées to the distant shadow of the Arc de Triomphe; the vast, soft-gray towers of Notre Dame, with its tortured gargoyles and magnificent portals leading to the splendid dimness inside; and in severe contrast, high on its hill, the startling whiteness of the Basilique du Sacré-Coeur, whose stones seem to grow whiter with age. And then there is the grossly modern Pompidou Center—the Beaubourg—blatantly displaying its enameled, gaudy pipework and plastic tubeways in the narrow, medieval streets of the Marais.

All this—and more—is there for you to seek out. Or, if you are one of the "idle people," you can sit outside one of the thousands of boulevard cafés, and simply watch the world go by.

Paris overview

Paris is an accessible city, pleasant and easy to walk around. Most of the larger streets—the avenues or boulevards—lead to a satisfyingly designed *place,* or square. Many of the smaller streets run adjacent to, or parallel to, these, so that even if you make a wrong turn you eventually arrive at a recognizable landmark.

Snaking through the middle of the city, flowing from east to west, is the Seine, dividing Paris into the Right (or north) Bank and the Left (or south) Bank. The river has dominated the city's history from the time when the first settlers, the Parisii, made the Ile de la Cité, today the site of Notre Dame, their home in the 3rd century B.C. From then on trade centered around the river and its two islands (the Ile St.-Louis is the other, smaller island). It is apt that the symbol of Paris is a ship.

Gradually, through the years of Roman occupation and the long night of the Dark Ages, the city grew. Notre Dame, the Louvre, the University, the Ste.-Chapelle, the Marais, the Bastille, and the Pont Neuf, all of them on or near the Seine, were among the earliest of the swelling city's monuments.

By the time Louis XVI was deposed, in 1792, Paris had grown magnificent under the Bourbon kings. They had added the place des Vosges, the Luxembourg Palace and Gardens, the Palais Royal, and the Académie Française. Louis XIV, the Sun King, oversaw the building of Versailles, Les Invalides, the Salpêtrière, Gobelins, the Louvre colonnade, and the Comédie Française. His successor's, Louis XV's, reign gave to Paris the Panthéon, the Palais-Bourbon, and the place de la Concorde.

On July 14, 1789, the Bastille was stormed and the Revolution began. Louis XVI and Marie-Antoinette, his queen, were executed in 1792, and the Reign of Terror began, instituted by the inscrutable, icy Robespierre, aided and abetted by Danton and Marat. 2,800 "enemies of the Revolution" in Paris alone were done to death by Dr. Guillotine's new machine. By 1794, however, Robespierre himself had been executed and Napoleon appointed First Consul. Under Napoleon, industry developed and the arts flourished. But the Corsican corporal, having spread the Revolution almost throughout Europe by virtue of his seemingly invincible Grand Armée, was himself defeated in 1815 at Waterloo, and the Bourbon monarchy was restored.

From 1815 to 1848 Paris underwent severe modernization. The Ourcq, St.-Denis, and St.-Martin canals were built. The first railway in France was laid down, running between Paris and St.-Germain-en-Laye. During the Second Empire, a further, even more wide-ranging, rebuilding program was put in hand, chiefly under the guiding hand of Baron Haussmann, but prompted by the ambitious, eccentric Napoleon III. Substantial areas were demolished as Haussmann drove his enormous and stately boulevards through the ancient city. The Opéra, Les Halles, Vincennes, and the Bois de Boulogne all took shape, as modern Paris emerged from the medieval city. It was now that the city was divided into its 20 *arrondissements,* or districts. 1855 saw the first Paris International Exhibition, followed by another in 1867, a showcase for the Second Empire.

Napoleon III's bungling caught up with him in 1870, however, when a newly-unified and aggressive Germany invaded France and captured Paris. But though the citizens were driven to eating rats—even the two elephants in the Botanic Gardens, Castor and Pollux, found their way onto Parisian menus—the city quickly recovered after the war and a new period of pomp followed. It culminated in the building of the Eiffel Tower—a "lonely suppository," as the writer Huysmans called it—and a great World Exhibition in 1889. The first line of the métro opened in 1900.

Paris escaped damage in World War I, but suffered much under the Nazi occupation 20 years later. Hitler's order to destroy the city, following the German retreat in 1944, was happily disobeyed by the German commander. The French—not least the Parisians—are justly proud of their Resistance fighters, many of whom carried on their secret war in the city's labyrinthine sewers, under the very feet of their conquerors.

PARIS MISCELLANY

Try to arrange your stay in Paris to coincide with the particular types of entertainment the city offers throughout the year. If, for example, you are keen on the theater, the opera, ballet, and art exhibits, there's not much point coming in August or the beginning of September. Practically the whole of Paris closes up shop then and heads off on vacation; even a good many restaurants are closed for two or three weeks during July and August. But if, on the other hand, you simply want to explore the city and its sights, August is an excellent time to visit, if sometimes very hot. The third week of September sees the start of the "artistic" season, with the pace heating up all the way through to Christmas. January and February, traditionally the dead months as far as tourism is concerned, can be an excellent time to visit, though it can be very cold.

Though the center of the city will certainly occupy most of your time—this is where the greatest concentration of monuments, museums, and other places of interest is found—there are also a number of fascinating and famous places of interest a little farther afield, all of them easily reached from Paris. Versailles, Fontainebleau, Vaux-le-Vicomte, Malmaison, St.-Germain-en-Laye, Chartres, Reims, Giverny, and Rouen are all well worth visiting, either for a day or a little longer. The Paris tourist office can help with travel arrangements.

The Eiffel Tower and Champs Elysées

As you stand underneath this giant tower, symbol of Paris the world over, trying to decide whether or not to climb it, think of its height—320 meters, or 1,051 feet—its weight—7,000 tons—and the 52 tons of paint used every seven years to paint it. Think of the 1,652 steps to climb if the elevators aren't working or you don't feel like paying the 40 frs. to take the elevator to the third stage. Think of the view, too; up to 42 miles on a clear day (the best time, so they say, is as near as possible to sunset). Then think of the idiot, home-made wings strapped to his back, who plummeted to an early grave from the summit. Think of the fool who rode his bicycle down from the first stage, and of the mad mountaineer who scaled it. But then think that you'll be able to go back home and tell your friends that you, too, went to the top of the Eiffel Tower. *Bonne Chance!*

Stages one and two open every day in summer from 10 in the morning to 11 at night; in the winter from 10:30 to 6. Stage three is open only in the summer, from 10 to

EIFFEL TOWER, CHAMPS ELYSÉES

6. There are elevators to all three stages (and stairs!), and long lines almost all year round. There's an excellent restaurant on the second stage, the **Jules Verne,** separate entrance from the Pilier Sud (south corner)—see 7th Arrondissement in the Restaurant listings—shops on all the stages, and a bar at the very top for those who want to get higher still.

From the Eiffel Tower, cross the Pont d'Iéna to the **Palais de Chaillot.** The building looks like something from 1930s Russia. Drink in the way the Palais and adjoining Trocadéro are aligned symmetrically with the Eiffel Tower and the Champs-de-Mars across the river, with the weighty facade of the École Militaire and, beyond that, the great dome of Les Invalides, under which Napoleon lies buried, as a backdrop. The broad terrace here is a marvelous place for taking photos of the tower and general river views. The Palais de Chaillot now houses several museums: the **Musée de l'Homme,** the **Musée de la Marine,** the **Musée des Monuments Français,** and the **Musée du Cinéma,** where you will get a guided tour by the movie-mad curator.

Opening times for the museums in the Palais de Chaillot are: Musée de la Marine daily 10 to 6 except Tuesday and public holidays; Musée de l'Homme daily 9:45 to 5:15 except Tuesday, film shows every day at 3 except Tuesday and Sunday; Musée des Monuments Français daily 9:45 to 12:30 and 2 to 5:15 except Tuesday; Musée du Cinéma daily except Monday for guided tours *only* at 10, 11, 2, 3, and 4.

If you're in the museum mood, walk along the avenue d'Iéna to the place d'Iéna, site of the **Musée Guimet.** The museum has some extraordinary Cambodian sculptures. But if Cambodian and Tantric Buddhist art leave you cold, try the **Musée d'Art Moderne** in the Palais de Tokyo opposite. Otherwise, walk right past the Guimet, carry on up the avenue d'Iéna to the Arc de Triomphe, and prepare yourself for another climb.

The Musée Guimet, 6 place d'Iéna, is open daily except Tuesday from 9:45 to 12 and 1:30 to 5:15. The Musée d'Art Moderne de la Ville de Paris, to give it its full name, in the Palais de Tokyo, is open 10 to 5:30 on

FUN IN PARIS 20

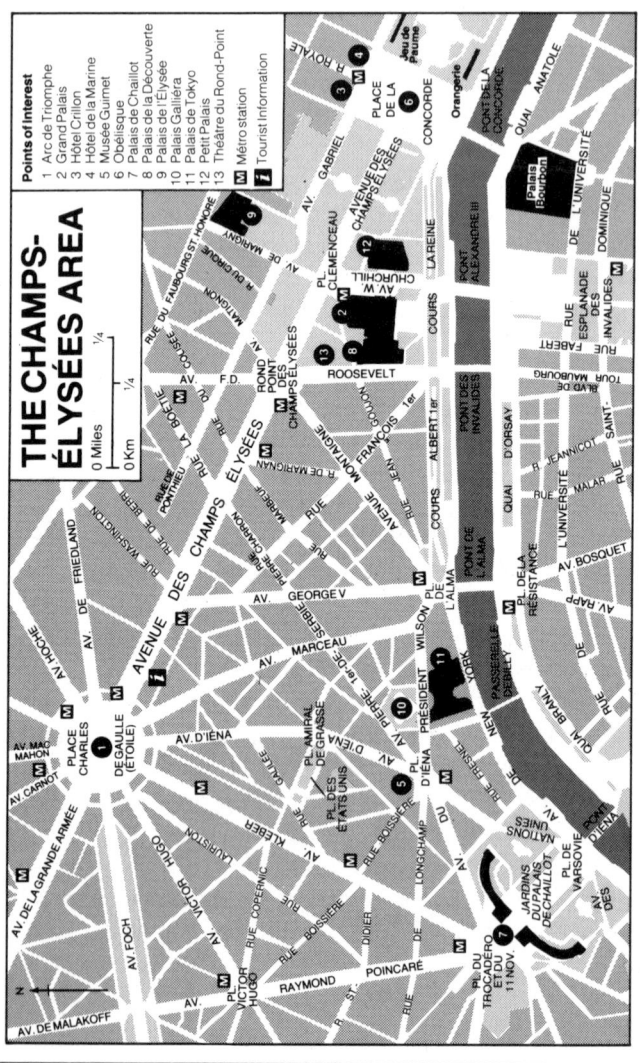

Tuesday and Thursday through Sunday, and 10 to 8:30 Wednesday, and is closed Monday.

THE ARC DE TRIOMPHE

They originally thought of building a vast stone elephant with an amphitheater, banqueting hall, and apartments *inside* it. But, at Napoleon's command, they built this arch instead. When his new empress, Marie-Louise, was due to make her triumphal entry into Paris in 1810, the Arch was only a few feet above the ground. They were having trouble with the foundations. So, with typical Gallic aplomb, a vast, painted canvas replica of the Arch was hoisted up on a huge scaffold. Rumor has it that this same scaffold had been used at Marie-Antoinette's execution.

Take in the monumental relief sculptures covering the Arch, the names of all Napoleon's victories inscribed around them. At ground level is the **Tomb of the Unknown Soldier** with its eternal flame. A flyer called Godefroy flew his plane through the Arch in 1919. Inside, you can listen to and look at an audio-visual history of the Arch (French and English). And, if you've recovered from climbing the Eiffel Tower, climb the Arc de Triomphe. The view down the Champs Elysées and over Paris is well worth it.

The Arc de Triomphe is open daily 10 to 5. There's a small extra charge for the audio-visual presentation and the elevator.

When you've done the Arch—and avoided those 12 death traps they call avenues, all of which converge here, by sensibly using the underpass—you are ready for the **Champs Elysées.** This incredibly wide avenue, offering one of the most spectacular views in Paris, is lined on both sides with banks, airline offices, cinemas, car showrooms, and multi-purpose centers such as **Point Show** at 68 and **Les Champs** at 84, where you can eat, drink, shop, and watch a movie all at the same time. There are also large shopping malls, where you can buy exclusive fashions; definitely for the well heeled. A number of prostitutes—also well heeled—operate here, but they are so chic you could easily confuse them with high society Parisians.

As you amble toward the Rond Point at the foot of the Champs Elysées, you pass avenue George V on your right. About four blocks down this street, on the left, is the **Crazy Horse Saloon.** You can't really miss it as it's next door to the **Théâtre de Champs Elysées** and an attractive little church called the Holy Trinity, presenting you with a convenient choice between God and the Devil. The Crazy Horse is slick and slinky and lots of fun, though a bit expensive at 250 frs. per person with two drinks, or 350 frs. for a table and two drinks. They also charge an extra 15% for service. The Théâtre is much less expensive. It was built in 1913 and houses a main theater, specializing in opera and concerts, and two other theaters: the Comédie des Champs Elysées, and the Studio des Champs Elysées. Entrance to this great complex is on avenue Montaigne.

Return to the Rond Point on the Champs Elysées, towards the place de la Concorde. On your left are another two theaters: the **Carré Marigny** and the **Petit Marigny.** Both are typical of the Parisian preference for revue.

Grab a snack if you're in the mood at **L'Hippopotamus,** 6 avenue Franklin-Roosevelt; it's cheap and cheerful, and has good steaks.

Opposite the Marigny is the **Grand Palais,** and, just down from that, the **Petit Palais,** two of the principal exhibit galleries in the city. Both are examples of the not-knowing-quite-where-to-stop school of architecture, especially the Grand Palais, a veritable Grande Dame of a building, overdressed and wearing all her finery.

The Grand Palais, avenue du Général-Eisenhower, is open Monday and Thursday through Sunday from 10 to 8, Wednesday from 10 to 10, and closed Tuesday. The Petit Palais on the avenue Winston Churchill is open Tuesday through Sunday 10 to 5.40.

When you re-emerge, walk down the avenue Winston Churchill to the Pont Alexandre III, the broadest bridge in Paris as well as one of the most beautiful. Built for the Great Exhibition of 1900, the bridge has everything that characterized the Belle Époque: style, class, power, exuberance.

Back on the Champs Elysées, you approach the

EIFFEL TOWER, CHAMPS ELYSÉES

place de la Concorde. It opens out magnificently in front of the **Tuileries Gardens,** with the **Jeu de Paume** behind it to the left, and the **Orangerie** to the right, both continuing the architectural symmetry that began back at the Arc de Triomphe. This dramatic panorama of buildings, monuments, fountains, and sculptures gradually gathers momentum as it nears the place de la Concorde where it bursts forth in a symphony of grand and elegant architecture, the whole revolving around the one anachronistic feature in the design, the massive, 3,300-year-old obelisk of Luxor, placed exactly in the center of the place de la Concorde. And you should see it at night. The Parisians really do have a right to boast about their beautiful city.

The Tuileries and the Louvre

From the place de la Concorde, the Tuileries Gardens stretch away to the east. In the distance you'll see the **Arc de Triomphe du Carrousel,** a scaled-down version of the Arc de Triomphe proper, at the west end of the Champs Elysées. Beyond it is the massive bulk of the Louvre whose arms enclose the new structure of the **Pyramid,** designed by the Chinese/American architect, I.M. Pei. Sit on one of those beautifully uncomfortable little metal chairs and soak it all in. It's one of the most amazing views in the whole city.

The **Jeu de Paume,** to the north, get its name from an early version of tennis that was popular in 17th and 18th-century France. It was long-famous as the Impressionist Museum, but, after extensive renovation and redecoration, it will be used to house temporary art exhibits. The fabled Impressionist collection (Manet, Monet, Degas, Gauguin, Renoir, Van-Gogh, Cézannne) has now been transferred to the new Musée d'Orsay on the other side of the river—(see page 61).

The **Orangerie,** the twin pavilion on the Seine side of the gardens, houses a fine collection of Impressionist and Modern art bequeathed to the French nation by a rich collector, as well as the superb **Water Lilies** series of paintings by Monet, the latter in a specially-built semi-circular gallery.

After this visit you might enjoy an ice cream and/or a drink at the open-air café in the heart of the Tuileries—metal seats optional—and prepare yourself to conquer the Louvre.

Louvre background

Built in 1200 by Philippe Auguste, the **Louvre** was originally a fortress on the banks of the Seine. It was only in the 14th century that Charles V converted it into a private residence. He also added a magnificent library. François I, a compulsive builder, carried out more conversions from about 1527, and also laid out the gardens. In 1546 François then commissioned the architect Lescot to build him a completely new palace on the site of the Louvre, but the king died before the work could begin.

Over the next 300 years the building was variously remodeled, renovated, lived in, and neglected by a succession of French monarchs, among them Henri II, Catherine de Médicis, Henri IV, Louis XIII, and Louis XIV, whose idea it was to turn the place into a museum. Louis, of course, had moved his court out to Versailles. In his absence the Louvre was taken over by a colony of artists, among them Boucher. Louis XIV expanded the palace to the east, building the beautiful **Colonnade du Louvre** and the perfectly-shaped **Cour Carrée,** the latter one of the most majestic parts of the whole complex.

Under Napoleon the palace was also expanded greatly, but the work came to a grinding halt with the restoration of the Monarchy in 1814. Louis XVII was the first of the restored kings, and the only French king to die in the Louvre. His successors didn't fare much better. Both Charles X and Louis-Philippe were expelled from the place by the French mob.

It was Napoleon III who finally completed the building. But in May 1871, during the bloody week of the Paris

Commune, insurgents set the place on fire, gutting the Marsan and Flore pavilions completely. Both were rebuilt under the Third Republic. This is how we see it today. Almost. A sci-fi transformation is taking place in front of the Louvre facing the Tuileries Gardens. It's a glass Pyramid that, when complete in 1989, will be the entrance to all the galleries. It will also house an extensive museum shop. The transformation includes the reconstruction of the Tuileries Terrasses on the west side.

LOOKING AROUND THE LOUVRE

The Louvre's catalog lists 300,000 items, give or take a few. If you manage to see 300 properly you will have done well, and can feel as proud as you did when you climbed to the top of the Eiffel Tower.

The **Grande Gallery** is on the second floor. It is the longest gallery in the world. It's 300 meters long, nearly 1,000 feet from the **Apollo Gallery** to the **Pavillon de Flore.** Begin at the Apollo Gallery. Look at the paintings first. You enter through the **Salles** (or "rooms") **Percier et Fontaine,** having passed the statue of *The Winged Victory of Samothrace* (best-known as the original of the little figure above the grille of every Rolls Royce) which, it is rumored, will find a new resting place in the glass Pyramid. You are now entering the realms of French 14th-century painting: the *Portrait of Jean le Bon* (1360) against a gold background is the first realistic portrait of a French king. On to the **Salon Carré,** where you will find the 15th-century *Avignon-Pietà,* a poignant and beautiful masterpiece. In the next small room, looking out over the Seine, are French 16th-century paintings. Then you arrive at **Grande Gallery,** where you see works by La Tour, Poussin, Claude Lorraine, Le Brun, and other 17th-century French masters. Turn right into the **Salle des États** for the Italian 16th-century and, of course, the *Mona Lisa.* You'll have to fight your way through crowds of supplicants to get a glimpse of her behind her reflective glass; better to concentrate on the Titians.

Pass behind the screen at the end, behind Veronese's enormous *Wedding at Cana,* into the **Salle Denon,** and then turn right into the **Salle Daru,** where you will be confronted by Géricault's dramatic *Raft of Medusa* and Delacroix's *Scenes of the Massacres of Chios.* Go back through the Salle Denon and into the **Salle Mollien** for more French neo-Classicism: David's great polemics and Ingres's ravishing nudes. At the end of this room you will pass an escape route in the shape of the Mollien staircase, but don't let it tempt you—go and have a cup of coffee in the restaurant instead.

Suitably refreshed, continue through the **Mollien Wing** and have a quick look at the paintings by Greuze before you rejoin the Grande Gallery. On your left are a number of Watteau's and Fragonard's delectable 18th-century scenes of courtly dalliance. On your right is one of the most splendid collections of Italian paintings assembled in one gallery: Giotto, Fra Angelico, Botticelli, Bellini, Guardi. In the midst of these you will find Flemish, Dutch, and German paintings from the 15th to 17th centuries. Be sure not to miss Rubens' heroic series illustrating the life of Catherine de Médicis. Its scale and imaginative power are breathtaking.

From now on you are on your own. The first floor houses Greek and Roman antiquities—including the *Venus de Milo*—as well as Egyptian and Oriental works. More Greek and Roman antiquities can be found on the second floor, grouped around the Cour Carré, as are the French Crown Jewels in the Apollo Gallery. Up on the third floor you'll find temporary exhibits and graphic art, and some more French and English 17th- to 19th-century paintings. Finally, on the first floor of the **Pavillon des Etats** and the **Pavillon de Flore,** there are substantial collections of French sculpture, dating from the early medieval period to the 19th century, and foreign sculptures, among them pieces by Cellini and Michelangelo.

The Louvre is open every day, 9:45 to 6, except Tuesday and public holidays. There's an entry fee of 20 fr.; Sunday is free. There are guided tours every day except Sunday at 10:30 and 3 from the Information Desk

FUN IN PARIS   28

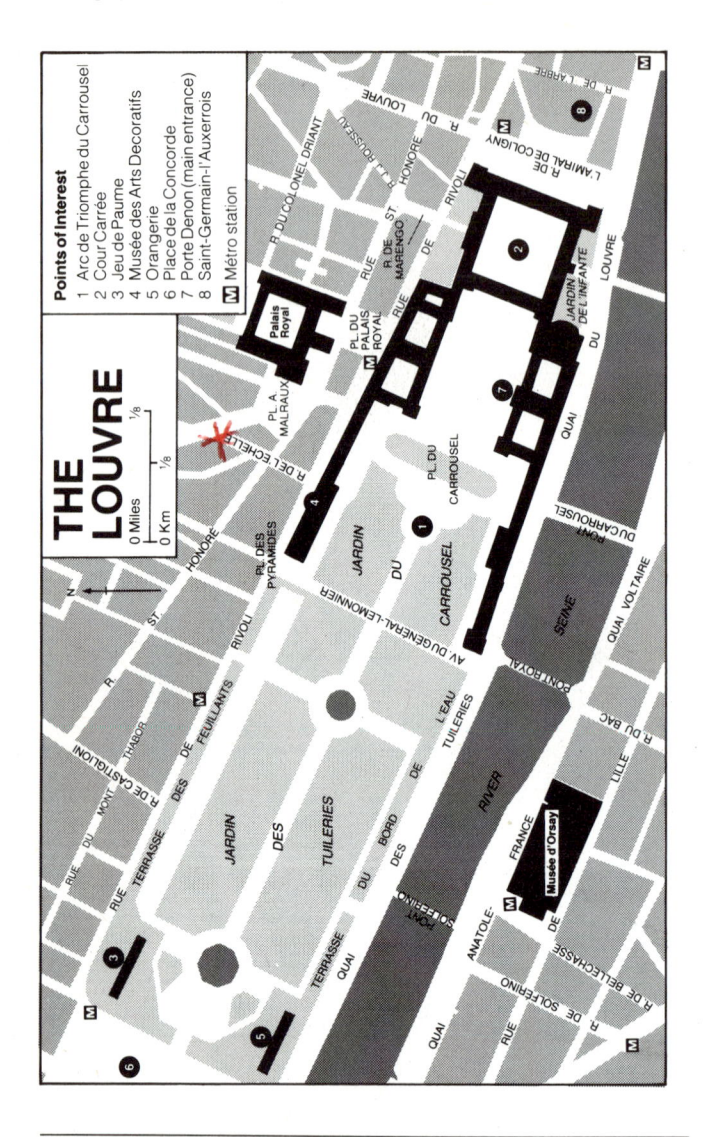

at the main entrance; 20–25 frs. Nearest métros are Palais Royal and Louvre.

Having successfully conquered the Louvre, you may like to head for an eating place! Try the rue St.-Honoré or around the place du Marché St.-Honoré. Both are filled with good restaurants offering a wide spectrum of specialties and prices.

Around the Opéra

This stage in our exploration of Paris begins at the **Palais Royal,** located immediately to the north of the Louvre. The Palais was built by Richelieu in the 17th century as his Paris residence—its size and sumptuousness give a potent idea of the power and wealth grabbed by the wily Cardinal. It subsequently passed into the hands of the regent Philippe, duke of Orléans, in whose tender care it became the scene of crazed revels and orgies. Thereafter it was owned by Philippe Egalité, duke of Orléans. Needing to raise money, he built a series of delightful town houses around the garden with first-floor arcades. These were intended as shops for the honest artisans of the city but quickly became the haunts of gamblers and prostitutes. Today, with the Palais Royal itself occupied by various government departments, the building and garden are respectability itself.

Despite their central location, the rose-filled gardens are an island of calmness and serenity, their elegant arcades providing welcome shade on a hot day. There's a pretty little fountain in the center of the garden and sandpits at the north end for children. You'll also find those ubiquitous little metal chairs, beloved by the

FUN IN PARIS

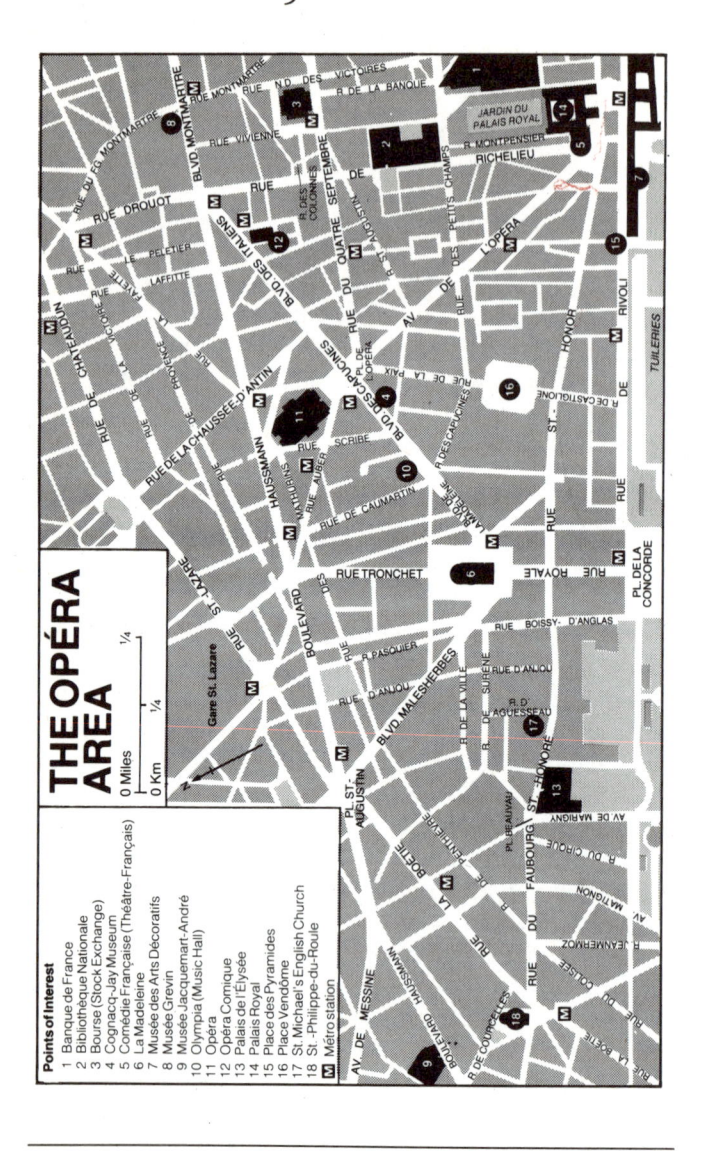

THE OPÉRA AREA

Points of Interest
1. Banque de France
2. Bibliothèque Nationale
3. Bourse (Stock Exchange)
4. Cognacq-Jay Museum
5. Comédie Française (Théâtre-Français)
6. La Madeleine
7. Musée des Arts Décoratifs
8. Musée Grevin
9. Musée Jacquemart-André
10. Olympia (Music Hall)
11. Opéra
12. Opéra Comique
13. Palais de l'Elysée
14. Palais Royal
15. Place des Pyramides
16. Place Vendôme
17. St. Michael's English Church
18. St.-Philippe-du-Roule
M Métro station

French municipal authorities. The **Montpensier Gallery** along the west side of the gardens contains several cafés and restaurants.

The first courtyard, if you enter from the south, is one of the talking points of Paris. It was transformed in 1986 into a huge piece of sculpture, designed by Duren.

31 AROUND THE OPÉRA

A small forest of black-and-white-striped stone pillars, checkerboard paving, and hidden lights and water, challenge the pompous pillars that surround the court with a series of perspective tricks. Like so many public displays of modernism in Paris, it's startling and done with great style. It also cost the earth to accomplish!

Leave the gardens at the north end and venture into the quaint and cobbled rue de Beaujolais, site of **Le Grand Véfour,** a gastronomic experience on the grand scale and, significantly less expensive, **Le Pullman,** a railroad-car of a restaurant. For full details, see First Arrondissement in the Restaurant listings.

You can make an intriguing detour here to the **Comédie Française.** Turn left down the rue de Montpensier, head past the little Théâtre du Palais Royal on the corner, and walk down the side of the Palais Royal to the place André-Malraux and the Comédie Française. The Comédie Française is the lone hub of traditional French comedy. The company doesn't restrict itself to comedy, however, and its repertoire also includes the likes of Racine and Corneille—in other words, all the heavyweights of French drama—plus a fair sprinkling of modern works both French and foreign. But, as befits an organization founded by Louis XIV—in 1680 to be exact, though it moved here only at the end of the 18th century —whose primary purpose was to spread far and wide the glories of the French stage, productions are still decidedly mannered and stagey. And of course in French.

Back on the rue de Beaujolais, head north up the little **passage des Deux Pavillons.** It's not much more than a flight of steps, and hardly altered over the centuries. This brings you onto the rue des Petits Champs. (Try the **Bistrot Vivienne** here—an excellent place for a snack). Heading right down the rue des Petits Champs you arrive at the **place des Victoires,** most beautiful of Parisian squares.

There's an equestrian statue of one LVDOVICO DECIMV OVARTO in the center of the square, gazing at a clutch of expensive clothes shops, among them Kenzo, Thierry, Mugler, and Victoire. Make your way back down the rue des Petits Champs and into the **Galeries Vivienne and Colbert.** They're a pair of covered shopping malls containing a miscellaneous array of antique and collectors' shops: books, coins, maps, medals, pipes, etc., which make an intriguing diversion. Nearby is the modern and charming **A Priori-Thé,** a tea-shop typical of the new vogue that's sweeping Paris.

Next to the Galérie Colbert is the **Bibliothèque Nationale,** the National Library. It houses one of the world's greatest collections of historical prints, manuscripts, engravings, photographs, medals, cameos, bronzes, coins, records, tapes, and talking machines, as well as about nine million books, the earliest dating from the 15th century, including a copy of every French book published since 1537. Here you will find two Gutenburg Bibles, first editions of Pascal, Villon, Rabelais, etc, Charlemagne's Gospel, and original manuscripts by the likes of Marie Curie, Victor Hugo, and Pasteur, to name but a few. Both the building and its contents are a veritable feast for the eyes. Take a look through the glass into the magnificent Second Empire Reading Room, with its cathedral-like domed ceiling and cast-iron columns.

The Bibliothèque Nationale entrance in the rue de Richelieu is open every day except public holidays from 12 to 6. The same entrance is used for exhibits. The entrance to the photography gallery is at 4 rue Louvois at the northwestern corner of the building.

Out of the Bibliothèque, continue north up the rue de Richelieu, crossing the rue St.-Augustin and the rue du Quatre Septembre, and turn right down the small, elegant rue des Colonnes. Here, at the end and to the left, you will find the public entrance to the **Bourse,** the Paris Stock Exchange. Don't be fooled by the classical serenity of the building. It's a madhouse inside. Head up to the public gallery from where the pandemonium on the floor is spread out below you: lunatics, all impeccably dressed, gesticulating wildly and shouting "J'ai!" or "Je prends!" at the top of their voices, speed around and jump up and down. These characters are the Wall Street wizards of Paris.

The Bourse is open Monday to Friday 11 to 2, with guided tours every half-hour; entry about 10 frs.

Not surprisingly, expense account lunching is the order of the day around the Bourse, and the area is packed with excellent, if expensive, restaurants. Try one and you may find yourself sitting next to one of the aforementioned maniacs. See Second Arrondissement in the Restaurant listings for full details.

For a very different type of eating experience walk up to the rue Feydeau, immediately north of the Bourse. Here, at #5 opposite the entrance to the passage des Panoramas, is a tiny old restaurant, apparently nameless. All that distinguishes it are the words "Restaurant Vins." You'd easily think you were walking into a private home as you push the door open. The food, like the atmosphere, is deeply traditional. The passage des Panoramas is itself full of small restaurants, ranging from inexpensive self-service joints, to the **Trattoria Toscana** for traditional Italian food, the **Mitidja Oriental** and, perhaps the most eccentric of all, the **Bistrot du Fort.** Here, it's the patron, bizarre ex-motor-bike champ Pierre Monneret, rather than the food, that's the main attraction. Again, full details, under Second Arrondissement, in the Restaurant listings.

Leave the passage des Panoramas and head into the busy boulevard Montmartre. Directly opposite is the **Musée Grévin,** the wax-works museum, so-called because it was founded by the caricaturist Grévin in 1882. This is a wonderfully tacky place to come to grips with Parisian history, with 20 kitsch scenes highlighting the building of the Eiffel Tower, the nightclubs of Montmartre, and a variety of exotic environments, each more ludicrous than the last. A grotto, complete with distorting mirrors, provides the *pièce de résistance.*

The Musée Grévin is at 10 boulevard Montmartre and is open Monday through Saturday 2 to 7, Sunday and public holidays 1 to 8; entry 30 frs.

As you walk west down the boulevard Montmartre, take the left fork and go down the boulevard des Italiens, passing the Salle Favart on your left, the second home of the Paris Opéra.

Continue down boulevard des Italiens and you arrive at the place de l'Opéra, where the **Palais Garnier,** the Paris Opéra house, is resplendent in all her overblown finery. The Paris Opéra has been resident in this magnificent building since 1872, when Charles Garnier completed his grand Napoleon III-style palace. Beneath the cellars is a submerged lake, den of the Phantom of the Opéra. Above, the facade is a riot of columns, friezes, winged figures, busts, and sundry ornamenation. Inside, the building is all marble, huge staircases, chandeliers, gilt decorations, caryatids holding up elaborate candelabra, tiers of arches, and galleries; then there is the room with parquet and mirrors, where spectators (of the Opéra and of each other) parade themselves in their Sunday best. On the subject of which, there's no point even trying to get into the Opéra for a First Night, a Gala, or a Subscription performance in anything less than a tux—"un smoking" as the French have it—or your best tiara.

THE MADELEINE AND PLACE VENDÔME

On the southwest corner of the place de l'Opéra on the boulevard des Capucines is one of Paris's most appealing small museums, one that will delight anyone with a taste for 18th-century painting. This is the **Musée Cognacq Jay,** a private museum packed with works by Boucher, Fragonard, La Tour, Canaletto, and Gainsborough.

The museum is open daily except Monday and public holidays from 10 to 5:40; entry fee is 10 frs., free on Sunday.

From here head down the boulevard des Capucines, which in turn becomes the boulevard de la Madeleine, to the place de la Madeleine and **La Madeleine** itself, or to give it its proper name, the Church of St. Mary Magdalen. It looks like a Greek temple but could just as easily have looked like a great many other things if the people connected with its early history had had their way. Two buildings were begun here—the first modeled on the Invalides, the second on the Panthéon—but both were razed to the ground when not much more than the foundations had been laid. Then, in 1837, when the present building was nearing completion, it almost became Paris's first railroad station. Happily it escaped this ignominious end, and in 1842 was finally consecrated. Fate had one further twist in store, however: in 1871 the rioting mobs of the Commune shot and killed the priest.

Walk all round the outside. It's a magnificent sight, with 52 giant Corinthian columns, each 66 feet high, supporting a powerfully sculptured frieze. From the top of the monumental flight of steps that leads to the main entrance there's an incredible view down the rue Royale to the place de la Concorde and on to the Palais Bourbon and the dome of the Invalides on the other side of the Seine. The huge, bronze doors are equally magnificent, with reliefs of the Ten Commandments. The interior is dim and somber, with the single nave crowned by three domes. There is a flower market next to the church, and some excellent food shops all round the square.

Crossing the rue Royale, just south of the place de la Madeleine, is the **rue du Faubourg St.-Honoré.** This is one of the most famous shopping streets in Paris, with St.-Laurent, Hermès, Lanvin, and Helena Rubinstein rubbing shoulders with art galleries (also on avenue Matignon), and antique shops. The fashion houses are situated mainly around the rue Royale and the rue de l'Elysée.

Going east along St.-Honoré you arrive at the **place Vendôme.** Originally there was a statue of Louis XIV in the center of the square. This was destroyed in the Revolution and replaced by the bronze column, modeled on Trajan's Column in Rome, commemorating Napoleon's victories in Germany. This, too, was pulled down during the Commune, then put back up again. Napoleon's statue is on the top, looking out at the jeering faces carved on the keystones over the arches around the square.

The place Vendôme was designed for Louis XIV by Jules Hardouin-Mansard. All the facades of the square are uniform, with arcades at ground level, Corinthian pilasters rising through two storys, and roofs with dormer windows. Chopin died at #12. Today, the square is filled with expensive shops, including great jewelers like Boucheron and Van Cleef & Arpel, art dealers, the Ministry of Justice, and the Ritz Hotel. They combine to create an almost palpable air of power, wealth, and beauty. It's very Parisian and very desirable.

THE GRANDS BOULEVARDS

The rue de la Paix heads northeast out of the place Vendôme. It takes you back to the place de l'Opéra and the Grands Boulevards: Capucines, Italiens, Montmartre, Poissonière, Bonne-Nouvelle, St.-Denis, and St.-Martin. The more easterly boulevards are now a bit down at heel and tawdry, so serious shoppers should head for the areas just north and southwest of the Opéra. Directly north of the Opéra is the **boulevard Haussmann,** an enormous thoroughfare where the traffic never seems to give way, stop or slow down. Haussmann was the man who razed half Paris to the ground between 1852 and 1870. His great redevelopment scheme was by no means all bad. Paris may have lost some of its old quarters and fine buildings, but it gained Les Halles, all its principal railroad stations, the Bois de Boulogne and Vincennes, the Opéra, the sewers, the completion of the Louvre, its 20 arrondissements and, of course, its boulevards. Far worse destruction has been seen in more recent times with the demolition of Les Halles, the thoughtless development of the expressway along the Seine, and the neglect of many beautiful old buildings outside the center of the city. One last word about Haussmann: when you walk down rue du Faubourg St.-Honoré take a look at the 12 steps that go *up* to the entrance of the church of St.-Roch. Before Big Baron Haussmann battered his way through, the entrance to this church was *down* seven steps.

There's a cluster of department stores round the back of the Opéra waiting for anyone who's managed to cross the boulevard Haussmann: Galeries Lafayette, Marks and Spencers, and Au Printemps (the top-floor restaurant here has *art-nouveau* decor and a wonderful stained-glass cupola).

South of the Opéra, down the **avenue de l'Opéra,**

AROUND THE OPÉRA

you'll find a further collection of elegant shops—jewelers, shoe stores, perfumers—and several good terrace restaurants and cafés. At the end of the avenue de l'Opéra is the Palais Royal and the Comédie Française—more or less where you started out.

From here the **rue de Rivoli** runs eastwards towards the Chatelet and the Hôtel de Ville, and westwards back towards the Tuileries and the place de la Concorde. Again, shopping is the major attraction here. Walk the length of the rue de Rivoli under the beautiful arcades past all types of luxury and souvenir shops. There is an elegant café or two if you begin to wilt, and you are never far from a métro station.

Montmartre

To reach Montmartre, take the métro to Anvers, head north up the little rue Steinkerque, and make a left at the place St.-Pierre. From here there are four routes. If you're feeling energetic, take the rue Foyatier and climb up the "Butte," the hill, to **Sacré-Coeur.** It's a beautiful climb but—be warned—very tiring. Alternatively, you can walk up through the gardens that lead directly to Sacré-Coeur. This is still quite a climb, but a good deal less exhausting. You can also take the rue Ronsard and the rue Paul Albert up on the east side of Montmartre. It's an attractive walk, with tiny cafés along the way. Finally, there's the easiest route of all. Take the funicular!

The name Montmartre is believed to be a corruption of *mont des martyres,* the mound of martyrs, a reference to the beheading here of St.-Denis in AD 250. (The story runs that St.-Denis subsequently marched, severed head in hand, to what is now the very much less than lovely district of St.-Denis about four miles north of Montmartre.) The name may equally well refer to a Roman temple to Mercury that is believed to have been here.

Be that as it may, Montmartre has always been a place apart from the rest of Paris, a fact that may well

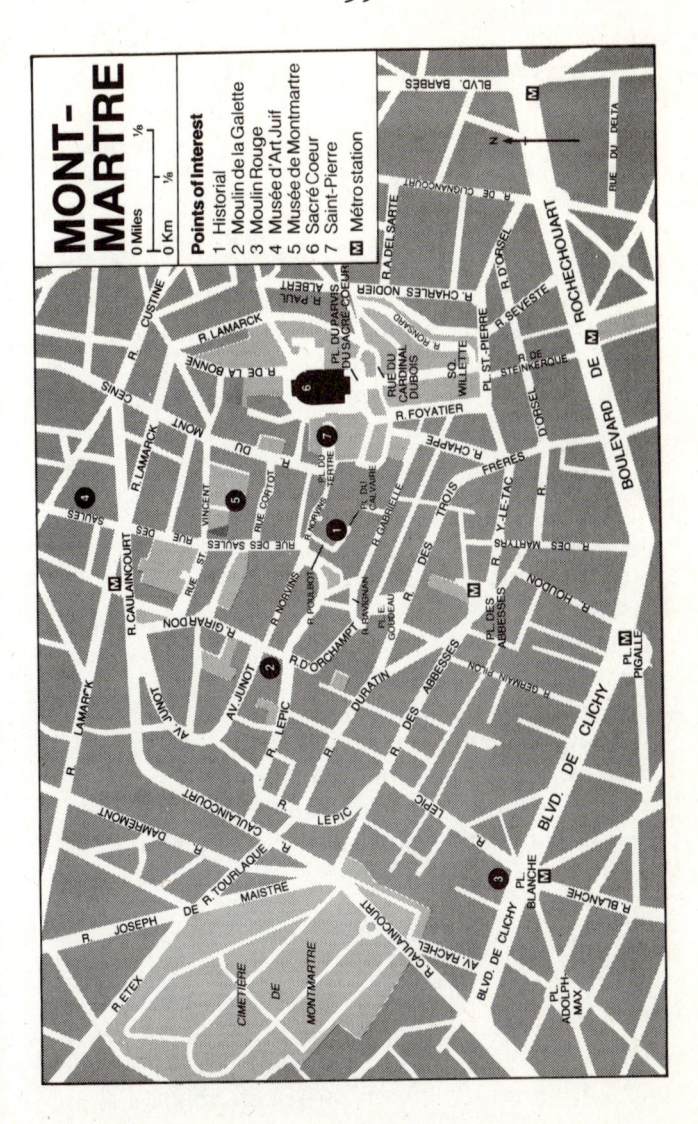

have accounted for its popularity among artists in the 19th and early 20th centuries. Before that, however, Montmartre—or the Butte, as the locals have it—was famous mainly for a Benedictine convent, founded in the 12th century. Henry IV, then king of Navarre, used it as his base when he tried to seize Paris in 1589. (As it turned out, his only conquest was the 17-year-old abbess.) In 1794, the convent was destroyed by the godless mobs of the Revolution, the last abbess was guillotined, and the name of the hill was changed to Mont-Marat, in honor of the man in the bath tub.

Today, of course, Montmartre is famous for three things. First, the basilica of Sacré-Coeur, built at the end of the Franco-Prussian war in 1870 as a symbol of national revival, and either hideous or beautiful (opinions have long been violently divided). Second, as an artistic quarter, full of painters and saucy Frenchmen in cafés. (In fact, though Montmartre once genuinely was the haunt of poets and painters, and the scene of bacchanalian revels that scandalized the bourgeoisie, these days any artistic activity is conducted on a strictly commercial basis for the exclusive benefit of the tourists who flock here in the vain hope of finding someone—anyone—who answers, however distantly, to the description of an artist.) Third, of course, there's the nightlife, covering the entire spectrum from the positively institutionalized respectability of the Moulin Rouge to the lowest of low lifers, lurking in doorways and dingy clubs.

At the top of the rue Foyatier steps make a right and you arrive at the Parvis du Sacré-Coeur. A short climb brings you to the gleaming white basilica. If you climb into the dome, there is a really magnificent view over Paris as well as a bird's eye view of the interior of the church.

Walk around the back of the church to the north side of the hill, and you enter a series of more peaceful streets, many of them rebuilt in the '20s. Beyond these, just over the rue Caulaincourt, is the **Musée d'Art Juif** at 42 rue des Saules. It's open Tuesday, Thursday, and Sunday from 3 to 6; closed on Jewish holidays and in August.

Back up the rue des Saules is the St.-Vincent cemetery, while farther west along the rue Caulaincourt is the **Montmartre Cemetery,** resting place of many of the famous people associated with Montmartre: Zola, Berlioz, Heine, Gautier, Dumas (fils), Degas, Offenbach, Stendhal, and Alphonsine Plessis, better known as The Lady of the Camellias or "La Traviata."

The southern end of the rue des Saules contains the only remaining vineyard in Paris, and **Le Lapin Agile,** a little café that was long one of *the* artistic rendezvous in Paris. Though inevitably commercialized now, it has survived surprisingly well. In fact, this little corner of Montmartre still exudes a village atmosphere quite unlike anywhere else in the city.

Just down from here in the rue Cortot is the **Musée de Montmartre.** The building was originally home to many artists. Today it is full of mementos from the district. It's open daily from 2:30 to 5:30, Sunday 11 to 5:30.

The southern end of the rue des Saules runs into a jumble of little streets which, in turn, lead to the busy place du Tertre. Here you will be approached about 60 times a minute to have your portrait sketched. If you do succumb, shop around first and only choose an "artist" when you can see him actually working.

There are countless small cafés and restaurants here, as well as numerous fast-food and sandwich bars, plus a few cabarets at night: **La Mère Catherine** and **Le Clairon des Chasseurs. Le Consultat** in the rue Norvins and **La Crémaillère** in the place du Tertre are both better than average.

More nightlife is found along the boulevard de Clichy, south of the twisty streets of Montmartre proper. But here even the vaguest attempt to be Parisian, artsy or "Bohemian" has been abandoned. This is Times Square dumped straight into Paris. That's not to say you'll find only clip joints, amusement arcades, and painted ladies among the neon and the glitter, but it's no place to linger with a full wallet. The **Moulin Rouge** is here on the place Blanche, and the **Folies Bergère** is directly south on the rue Richer about half a mile away. Both are still going strong and presenting ever more lavish shows à la Vegas for the benefit of tourists from all over the globe (the Moulin Rouge recently, until the animal welfare people stepped in, had a dolphin leaping from a tank to pluck the clothes from a girl perched above it). But La Belle Époque it is not.

However, this corner of the world does boast one little cultural highlight, the **Musée Gustave Moreau.** This is in the rue de la Rochefoucauld, south of the place

Pigalle. Moreau, leading light of the Symbolist movement, lived here for 46 years until his death in 1898. Anyone interested in the wilder flights of late 19th-century Romanticism should take a look. The museum is open Wednesday to Sunday from 10 to 1 and 2 to 5, but closed on public holidays.

If you feel like a complete change, take the métro to Jaurès, a mile or more to the east, and walk down the avenue Secrétan to the **Parc des Buttes Chaumonts**. Here you can relax in the surprisingly romantic park, laid out—by Haussmann—on the site of a disused quarry. Steeply-sloping woods, a lake with a rocky island, numerous walks, and a good restaurant—the **Pavillon du Lac** —complete the picture.

On the other side of the Jaurès métro stop is the **St.-Martin canal,** built to link the Seine with the Ourcq canal. It is still a working canal, and the stretch between Frédéric Lemaitre square and the rue Bichat transports the onlooker into Amsterdam. It is serene, leafy, and picturesque, with hump-backed bridges. Boat trips along the canal are organized by Quiztour, 19 rue d'Athènes 9e (tel. 46-74-75-30/1).

Finally, for another short detour, head down to the **Musée Edith Piaf** in the rue Crespin-du-Gast in the 11th arrondissement (nearest métro is Ménilmontant). Memorabilia, clothes, and photos have all been lovingly assembled by fans of "La Môme de Pigalle" to form a moving display. Visits by appointment only: tel. 43-55-52-72.

The Beaubourg and the Marais

The walk around this neighborhood begins with the Forum Shopping Complex and the Beaubourg, two of the most modern buildings in the city. It then covers the Marais, most elegant of the city's aristocratic quarters. It is a walk in which history and modernity lie cheek by jowl.

THE FORUM AND THE BEAUBOURG

Running north between the Forum and the Beaubourg, or the **Centre National d'Art et de Culture Georges Pompidou,** to give its full name, is the boulevard de Sébastopol. To the west of it is the Forum, to the east is the Beaubourg.

The **Forum,** opened in the early '80s, stands on the site of Les Halles, Haussmann's great 19th-century food market. Built largely below ground level, it's packed with excellent shops, cafés, and restaurants. Architecturally, however, it leaves a great deal to be desired, not least in comparison to the magnificently atmospheric cast-iron-and-glass food market it replaced. Still, though the building may be unpleasant, the shopping's good. The last part of the Forum opened in 1987. This boasts new boutiques, a tropical garden, an auditorium, and an Olympic-sized swimming-pool.

For a glimpse of history before you come to grips with more ultra-modernity, walk up the boulevard de Sébastopol a couple of blocks and turn right into the rue du Bourg l'Abbé, which in turn becomes the rue Montmorency. Here, on your right at #41, is the house of **Nicholas Flamel.** Built in 1407 as a charitable institution, it's reputed to be the second-oldest house in the city (the oldest is just round the corner in the rue Volta, but it's very much less interesting to look at and is, in any case, a private residence). Flamel made his fortune through alchemy, and his house has now been lovingly transmuted into a cosy restaurant offering excellent traditional French cuisine.

Continue down the rue Montmorency, turn right into the rue Beaubourg, and head down to the Beaubourg itself. By now you are surrounded by acrobats, fire-eaters, fakirs, singers, clowns, break-dancers, performing dogs, budgerigars, monkeys, hippies, beatniks, punks, groupies, debs, androids, and tourists. The occasional, confused Frenchman can sometimes be spotted in the right season.

Before leaving this motley crew and heading into the Beaubourg itself, walk down to the right-hand side of the building and take a look at the Stravinsky Fountain, an intriguing specimen of "clockwork" art. Down this side and along the back you will see the design element that has made the Beaubourg such a controversial structure. All the pipes and ducts that carry the building's services are on the *outside,* brightly painted, instead of being inside and hidden.

The main entrance to the Beaubourg is at the base of the slope of the square. Inside, you will find the central information desk and a good museum shop. On the left as you go in is the Salle d'Actualité de la Bpi. Choose a record and a seat, hand over the numbers, and you can listen to your record for as long as you like.

You are in one of the most popular buildings in Europe. Be prepared to stand in line for some time before even being allowed onto the escalator which will take you up to the exhibition floors—safety regulations do not allow more than 4,300 people in the building at any one time.

The principal attraction is the Modern Art Museum, housed on the top floor. It's intelligently arranged, and in every way a magnificent collection. The museum also presents a considerable number of temporary exhibits every year, many of them of the highest quality. But the Beaubourg is more than just a museum. It fulfills an important role as a place of learning and study, charting, and in some cases instituting, every twist and turn in the shifting, enormously complex, and mysterious world of contemporary art. It's a vital, living barometer of modern culture.

While one can unreservedly applaud the work of the Beaubourg and its innovative and frequently challenging approach, the building in which this all takes place, itself widely applauded when opened back in the late '70s, is another matter.

The Beaubourg is open Monday and Wednesday through Friday from 12 to 10 P.M. and Saturday and Sunday from 10 to 10 P.M. It's closed on Tuesday and free on Sundays. The nearest métro is Rambuteau.

THE MARAIS

Walk north around the Beaubourg and take the rue Rambuteau east (buy yourself some tasty pastries, and croissants, or some fresh fruit, here). Turn left into the rue des Archives. You are now in the heart of the Marais.

On your right is the Hôtel de Soubise, which, with its neighbor, the Hôtel de Rohan, houses the magnificent collection that is the **French Archives:** 280 kilometers— a staggering 175 miles—of shelving containing the wills

FUN IN PARIS 46

Points of Interest
1 Basilique Notre Dame des Victoires
2 Beaubourg (Centre Pompidou)
3 Bibliothèque de l'Arsenal
4 Bourse du Commerce (Commodities Exchange)
5 Colonne de Juillet
6 Forum
7 Les Halles
8 Hôtel de Beauvais
9 Hôtel de Béthune-Sully (Caisse Nationale des Monuments Historiques)
10 Hôtel de Rohan
11 Hôtel Salé
12 Hôtel de Sens (Bibliothèque Forney)
13 Hôtel de Ville
14 Marais Cultural Center
15 Memorial du Martyr-Juif Inconnu
16 Musée Carnavalet
17 Musée de la Chasse
18 Musée de la Serrure
19 National Archives
20 Notre-Dame-des-Blancs-Manteaux
21 Place des Vosges
22 Saint-Eustache
23 Saint-Gervais-Saint-Protais
24 Saint-Merri
25 Saint-Paul-Saint-Louis
26 Square des Innocents
27 Tour Saint-Jacques
M Métro station

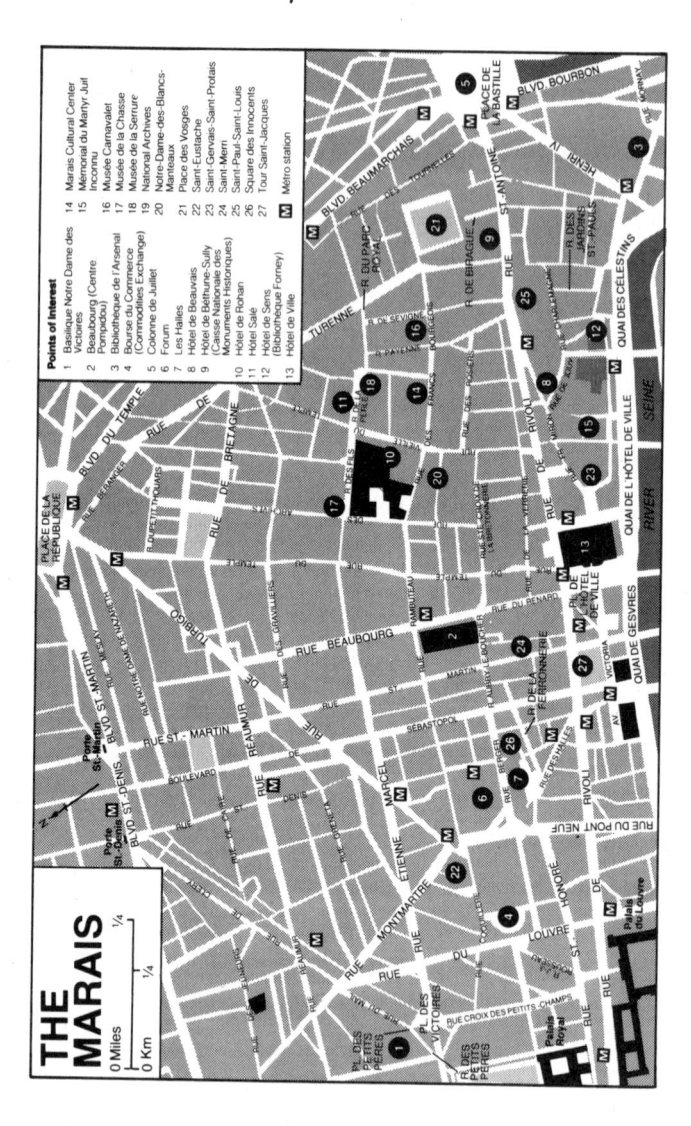

of Louis XIV and Napoleon, the Declaration of the Rights of Man, letters from Voltaire and Joan of Arc, and much, much more. Both the museum and the sumptuously-decorated apartments can be visited. They're open Monday through Sunday—closed Tuesday—from 2 to 5. The Hôtel de Rohan is also closed in July and August.

THE BEAUBOURG AND THE MARAIS

A little farther up the rue des Archives is the **Musée de la Chasse,** the Hunting Museum. The museum itself is only of secondary interest, but the building and formal garden are delightful. (Apply to the museum for permission to see the garden: tel. 42-72-86-43).

Go down the rue 4 Fils and turn left into the rue de Thorigny. Here, housed in what was originally the Hôtel Salé, is the **Musée Picasso,** the first museum dedicated entirely to the maverick Spanish master, and, with the Beaubourg and the Musée d'Orsay, one of Paris's top tourist attractions. The collection consists mainly of works Picasso kept for himself, but it's far from being just a series of sketches or false starts that he couldn't sell. Quite the opposite, in fact. It contains some superb works, including some very unusual sculptures, that for one reason or another Picasso refused to part with. In addition, Picasso's personal collection of paintings and drawings by friends and contemporaries—Braque, Matisse, Miró, and others—is also on show. The icing on the cake is provided by the building itself, a marvelous mid-17th century town house that took an astonishing ten years to restore. Don't miss it.

The museum, at 5 rue de Thorigny, is open daily, except Tuesday, from 10 to 5:15.

A few blocks south of the Musée Picasso is the **Musée Carnavalet,** at 23 rue de Sévigné. This, too, is a delightful building, with a collection illustrating every phase of Parisian history and architecture. It's open every day except Monday from 10 to 5:40, and is free on Sundays.

From the Musée Carnavalet, head down the rue des Francs Bourgeois to the **place des Vosges,** a haven of trees, arcades, and elegant architecture. The square dates from the early 17th century, from the reign of Henri IV, at whose command it was laid out. #6 is today the **Musée Victor Hugo,** full of memorabilia of the great French writer. It's open every day (except Monday) from 10 to 5, and is free on Sundays. For a good cup of coffee and a bite to eat, try **Ma Bourgogne** in the northwest corner of the square. Meals are served all day long.

Head south out of the place des Vosges, and turn right into the rue St.-Antoine. A block or two along, turn right up the little rue Pavée. This brings you to the rue des Rosiers and the **Jewish quarter.** Although the district is superficially down at heel, the true heart of the Marais continues to beat in its narrow streets. One of the few kosher restaurants in Paris is here—**La Rose Daisy;** full details in the Restaurant listings under 4th Arrondissement—while for snacks try the **Villette St.-Paul.**

The east end of the rue de Rivoli is just south of here, with an intriguing ice cream and fruit bar, opposite the tiny rue des Mauvais Garçons, beckoning you. It's called **Afruitisiaque**—the French have an appalling genius for coining names—and has a sensational line in ice cream. But if you can resist the siren call of Afruitisiaque, there is, on the Ile St.-Louis, probably the best ice cream shop in the city, of which more in a moment.

From here, head over the rue de Rivoli to the **Hôtel de Ville,** the City Hall, in the place de l'Hôtel de Ville. The building is a 19th-century copy of the original 16th-century building—this was burned down during the Commune in 1871—and the seat of the city government. Inside there's a veritable feast of extravagant painting and decoration. It's open Monday to Friday 8:45 to 6:30, and Saturday 9 to 6. There are guided tours of the salons on Mondays at 10.

The Ile St.-Louis and Ile de la Cité

Begin with the **Ile St.-Louis,** smaller of the two islands in the Seine. Predominantly residential, it is a delightful place to stroll, either along the quays or down the rue St. Louis-en-l'Ile that runs through the center. Here you will find the church of the same name, a number of good shops and restaurants, and, at #31, **Berthillon,** *the* ice cream shop. You can't possibly try all the flavors, but cram in as many as you can manage. If necessary, come back every day. They also supply little boxes in which the ice cream will last at least as long as it takes to go to the Tuileries on foot. (There's a chance that Berthillon's ice cream, securely packed in one of their little boxes, might make it to New York by Concorde, if the traffic to Paris airport isn't too bad). Berthillon ice cream can also be found in one or two shops in the rue des Deux-Ponts.

If you prefer tea, there is the **Salon du Thé St.-Louis** at #81, and, if you prefer beer and rugby players, there is the **Brasserie de l'Ile St.-Louis** beside the Pont St.-Louis. Nearby are some magnificent patisserie shops.

FUN IN PARIS   *50*

ILE DE LA CITÉ

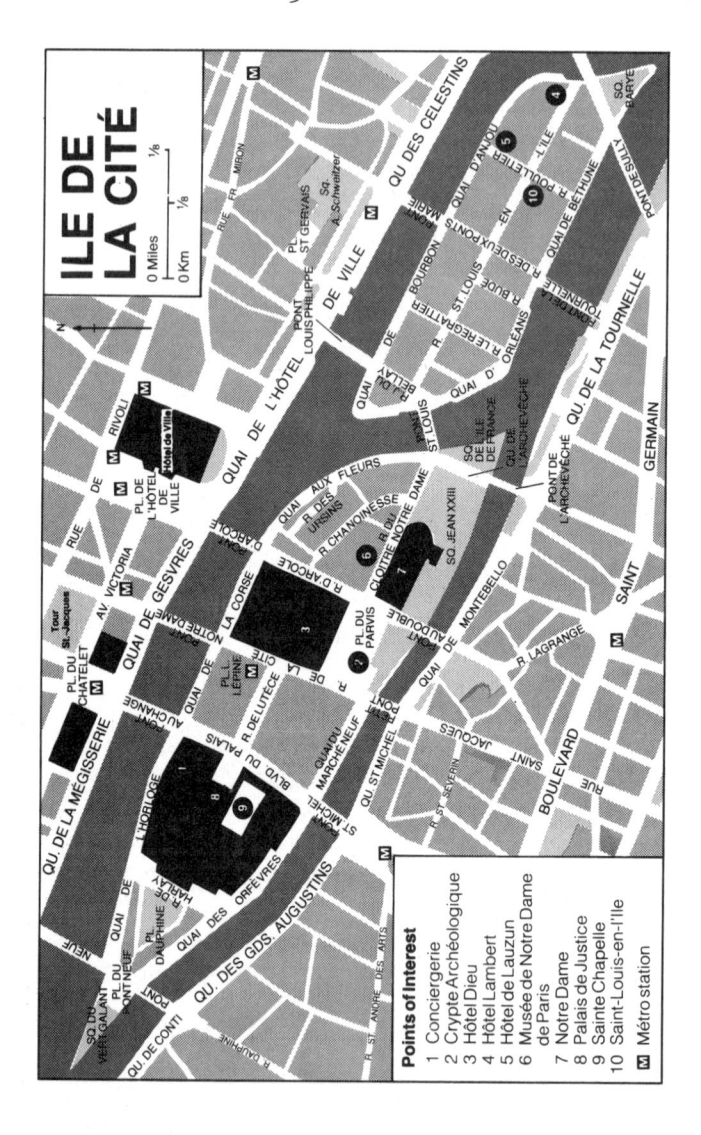

Points of Interest
1 Conciergerie
2 Crypte Archéologique
3 Hôtel Dieu
4 Hôtel Lambert
5 Hôtel de Lauzun
6 Musée de Notre Dame de Paris
7 Notre Dame
8 Palais de Justice
9 Sainte Chapelle
10 Saint-Louis-en-l'Ile

M Métro station

To get to the **Ile de la Cité,** cross over the little Pont St.-Louis at the west end of the Ile St.-Louis. Here you will find much more bustle, and much more to see. To put it another way, this is a place for serious sightseeing.

The three principal attractions on the Ile de la Cité are Notre Dame, the Conciergerie, and the Sainte-Chapelle. These are buildings that overawe through their sheer scale, and historical and architectural grandeur. They are somber, beautiful, magnificent, and unforgettable. This is as it should be, for you are now in the very heart of the city. Mind you, you won't be alone, for the Ile de la Cité draws tourists in much the same way as the Beaubourg or the Eiffel Tower.

Notre Dame dates from 1163, and was largely complete by 1250. Most of the sculptures on the facade are 19th-century replicas, many of the originals—particularly those representing the 28 kings of Israel—having been hacked down in the Revolution when they were erroneously identified with the French royal family. (Similarly, the spire, or *flèche,* over the chancel was also added in the last century). The three doorways are, from left to right, the Portal of the Virgin (the central sculpture here, the Virgin and Child, *is* original, and dates from the 13th century), the Portal of the Last Judgement, and the Portal of St.-Anne. Above them is the famous rose window. To bask in the shimmering pools of light and color it creates, step inside the building.

The massive 12th-century columns of the nave stretch away from you to the transepts—the "arms" of the church—and the chancel, or choir. A good part of the glass in the fabulous rose windows of the transepts is original. The chancel owes much of its appearance to a vow made by Louis XIII in 1638. Childless after 23 years of marriage, he promised to dedicate the whole of France to the Virgin Mary if his queen provided an heir. An heir was duly produced, and the king, by way of thanks, had statues of himself and his son—the future Louis XIV—placed in the chancel, as well as new choir stalls. To the south of the choir is the old sacristy, now the treasury, with a display of chalices and other ecclesiastical objects and manuscripts. There is also a nail and a splinter of wood, reputedly from the True Cross. These are produced on Sundays in Lent and on Good Friday.

If you're feeling hale and hearty, make your way to the north aisle near the Portal of the Virgin and climb the 387 steps to the summit of the north tower. From here, in the company of a series of grotesque gargoyles and other carved monsters, including the famous "striga" or vampire, who, chin in hands, passively contemplates the city's roof tops, you can cross over to the south tower. Visit the 13-ton bell here. It's still rung on special occasions.

At the west end of the Ile de la Cité is the **Palais de Justice,** the city law courts. It's open to the public so you can wander around the corridors watching the important-seeming bustle of the law-givers, or even attend a court hearing. But the major points of interest here are the Sainte-Chapelle and the Conciergerie.

The **Sainte-Chapelle,** hidden inside a courtyard of the Palais de Justice, is a stunning jewel case of a building. It was put up by Louis IX, otherwise known as Saint Louis (the genial and pious monarch was canonized 27 years after his death). Having purchased what he took to be the original Crown of Thorns from the Emperor Baldwin II of Constantinople, Louis resolved that a suitable shrine should be built to house it. The Sainte-Chapelle, completed in 1248—airy and diaphanous, glowing with light from its sensational stained glass—was the result. The lower half is somewhat gloomy these days, but the upper chapel remains among the city's most precious treasures. To see it at its most magnificent you should try to attend one of the candlelit concerts held at frequent intervals.

The Sainte-Chapelle is open every day from 10 to 5; half-price on Sunday.

The **Conciergerie**—a building that can be described as grim at best—forms the northeastern corner of the great complex of buildings here. Originally, it was part of the royal palace, but it is probably best known as the prison from which Marie Antoinette was taken to the guillotine. The name of the building derives from the fact that it was originally presided over by the governor, or concierge, of the royal palace. His considerable income was greatly increased by the special privilege he enjoyed of leasing out the shops and showrooms that once lined the first floor. The most distinctive features of the building are its four towers overlooking the Seine, the most famous of which is the Tour de l'Horloge, the Clock Tower, on the corner of the boulevard du Palais. The clock itself has been ticking away since 1370, and is the oldest public clock in the city.

You'll have to take a tour if you want to visit the inside, but it's well worth it. The splendid guardroom, with Gothic vaulting and columns decorated with intricately-carved capitals, and the huge Salle des Gens d'Armes are among the highlights. But you can also see the prisoners' gallery, various cells (including the one where Marie Antoinette was incarcerated), and the chapel. Highlifers should note that the kitchens, boasting four of the largest fireplaces you're likely to encounter anywhere, can be rented out should you have a yen to throw a really memorable party.

The Ile de la Cité has no shortage of tourist-type cafés and restaurants where you can get a moderately good bite to eat. Among the best are the **Bar du Caveau** and **Chez Paul,** both on the place Dauphine at the western end of the island overlooking the river.

The Left Bank

Begin your exploration of the Left Bank at the northern end of the boulevard St.-Michel, opposite the Ile de la Cité, by the Pont St.-Michel. This is the Latin Quarter. The name comes from the fact that this area of the city has long been the student quarter. As Latin remained the official language of education right up to the Revolution, so the area got its name. Head south down the boulevard St.-Michel, past the many bookshops and cafés, to the boulevard St.-Germain. To your right is St.-Germain itself; to your left the **Musée de Cluny.** Make a bee line for the museum.

It's housed in one of the few medieval houses—as opposed to public or religious buildings—left in the city. It was built for the monks of the rich and influential Cluny Abbey in Burgundy as their Paris HQ. Intriguingly, it stands on the site of the city's original Roman baths, impressive sections of which can be seen. The museum has a fine collection of medieval arts—statuary, jewelry, furniture, religious artifacts—the pearl in the collection being the superb *Dame à la Licorne* tapestries, a highly allegorical, late-medieval series of tapestries whose exact meaning has long since been lost. Their curious ambiguity only makes them all the more appealing, however. The museum also contains a number of the original 13th-century statues from the facade of Notre Dame. The museum is open daily, except Tuesday, from 9:45 to 12:30, and 2 to 5:15. Half price on Sunday and public holidays.

Leaving the Musée de Cluny, you'll see the gray bulk of the **Sorbonne** in front of you, the city's principal university building. It was founded by one Robert de Sorbon, from whom it takes its name.

Behind the Sorbonne head up the rue St.-Jacques to the forbidding mausoleum called the **Panthéon.** Beneath its vast dome are buried such illuminati as Voltaire, Rousseau, and Victor Hugo. This spendidly gloomy classical structure also contains a number of interesting murals, the most famous of which illustrates the story of Ste.-Geneviève, patron saint of Paris, and one-time shepherdess. The Panthéon is open every day from 10 to 12 and 2 to 4 (it is closed on Tuesday and public holidays, half price on Sunday).

You can make a substantial detour from here if you like plants and animals. This is to the **Jardin des Plantes,** the botanical gardens, about half a mile to the east of the Panthéon. Despite an excellent Natural History museum and a charming, decidedly old-fashioned zoo, the gardens are not on the tourist's beaten path, but they are worth a quiet visit.

From the Panthéon, back again on our main route, walk down the rue Soufflot to the boulevard St.-Michel, which here runs down past the **Jardin du Luxembourg.** There is a cluster of little cafés and restaurants where, for the price of no more than a cup of coffee, you can sit for hours and watch the endless procession of people up and down the boulevard St.-Michel.

The gardens of the **Luxembourg Palace** are delightful, an oasis of greenery among the traffic-thronged streets. The Palace itself was built by Marie de Médicis, who, born and raised in Florence's Pitti Palace, intended it to resemble her childhood home. After serving as a prison in the Revolution, it became in turn the seat of the Directory and the Consulate. Today it is the Senate, France's Upper Chamber. There is, however, little of

FUN IN PARIS   56

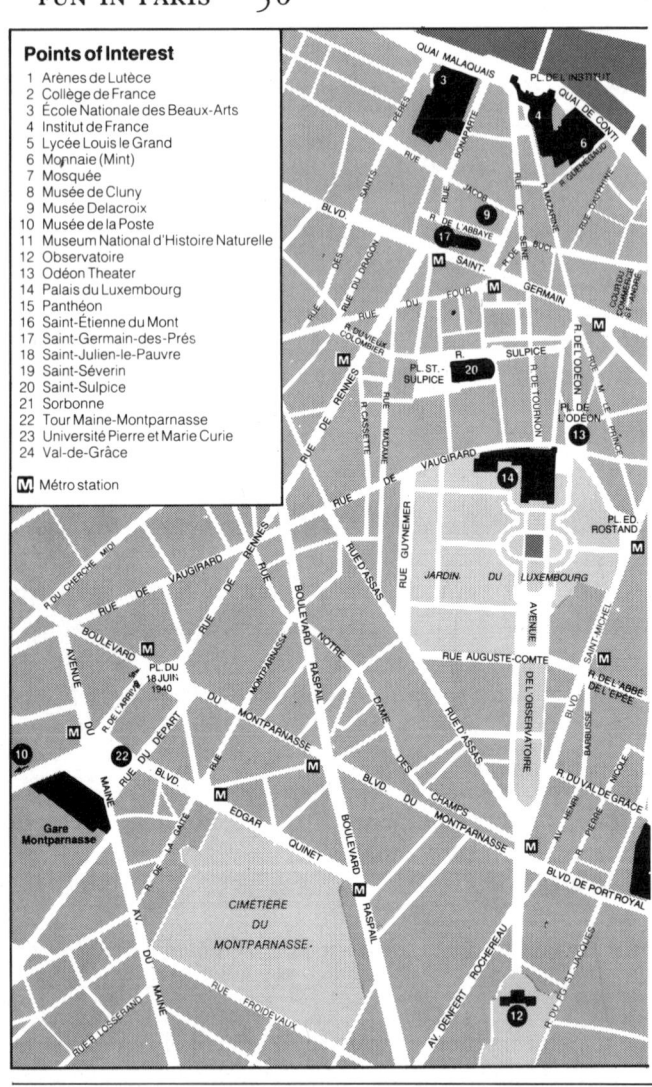

Points of Interest

1. Arènes de Lutèce
2. Collège de France
3. École Nationale des Beaux-Arts
4. Institut de France
5. Lycée Louis le Grand
6. Monnaie (Mint)
7. Mosquée
8. Musée de Cluny
9. Musée Delacroix
10. Musée de la Poste
11. Museum National d'Histoire Naturelle
12. Observatoire
13. Odéon Theater
14. Palais du Luxembourg
15. Panthéon
16. Saint-Étienne du Mont
17. Saint-Germain-des-Prés
18. Saint-Julien-le-Pauvre
19. Saint-Séverin
20. Saint-Sulpice
21. Sorbonne
22. Tour Maine-Montparnasse
23. Université Pierre et Marie Curie
24. Val-de-Grâce

M Métro station

interest inside, and it is in any case open only on Sundays. The gardens, with their Punch and Judy shows, fountains, and statues, are very much more diverting.

The southern end of the gardens leads to the **Paris Observatory,** where, on the first Sunday of each month at 2:30 in the afternoon, you can contemplate the cosmos (apply in writing to the Secretary, L'Observatoire, 61 avenue de l'Observatoire, 14e.).

THE LEFT BANK

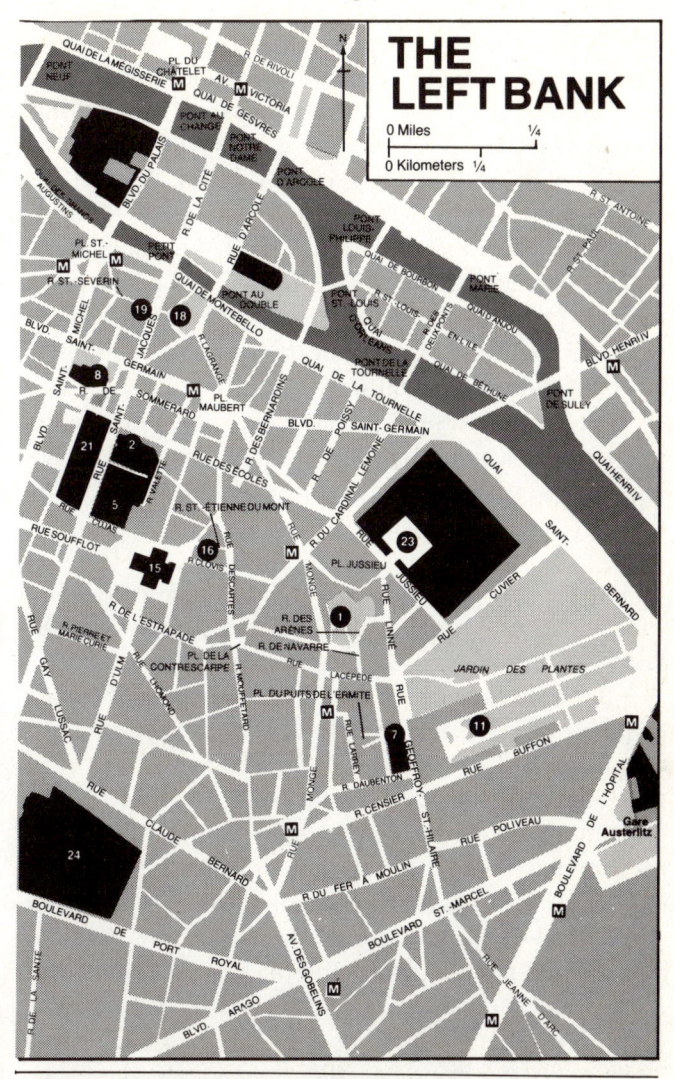

From here, if you still have any energy left—the area is liberally provided with restaurants, cafés, and bars for those in need of refreshment—a side trip to Montparnasse is in order. You can either walk up the boulevard du Montparnasse or take the métro to the aptly named Montparnasse Bienvenue.

Montparnasse has long been known chiefly as a district of poets and painters. Today, however, it is an area of towering skyscrapers and large modern hotels. But don't despair, the old Montparnasse is still there, struggling to survive and well worth seeking out. You'll never be short of entertainment, with movie theaters, café-theaters, and all the famous bars and cafés—of which more in a moment—still very much in evidence.

Begin your visit in the place du 18 Juin, 1940. Its curious name commemorates the date of de Gaulle's famous radio appeal to all Frenchmen, broadcast from London just after the fall of France. Towering over the square is the **Tour Maine-Montparnasse,** a dull hulk of steel and concrete, all 59 stories of it. It also has what is claimed to be the fastest elevator in Europe, which is well worth taking for the amazing view of the city. The building's open every day from 9:30 A.M. to 11:30 P.M. April through September, and 10 A.M. to 10 P.M. October through March.

At its base is the Commercial Shopping Center, a substantial modern mall that includes a branch of the famous Galeries Lafayette department store.

But if, like most visitors to Montparnasse, it's a spot of relaxed entertainment that has drawn you, head for the rue de la Gaîté. It's been crammed with dance halls, theaters, nightclubs, and restaurants since the 18th century. Inevitably perhaps, though it's nothing like as bad as Montmartre away to the north of the city, there's a degree of sleaze among the glamor, so be on your guard.

Alternatively, back on the boulevard du Montparnasse, you'll find the **Dôme** and the **Coupole,** both substantial café/brasseries, once the haunt of Hemingway, Joyce, Modigliani, Pound, Cocteau, and a whole host of lesser poets and painters earlier this century when Paris really was the artistic capital of the world. Among the supporting cast of thousands in those days was Lenin, too, though it's hard to imagine that he added much to the fun. At the far end of the boulevard du Montparnasse is the romantically named **Closerie des Lilas.** Today it's principally just a rather expensive restaurant, but you can still have a drink here and dream of the days when this pretty spot was a center of bohemianism à la Parisienne.

St.-Germain

St.-Germain is north of the Palais de Luxembourg and west of the boulevard St.-Michel. It's a haunt of artists, intellectuals, and writers rather than a sightseeing area as such. Only the two churches of **St.-Germain-des-Prés,** the only Romanesque or pre-Gothic church in the city, and **St.-Sulpice,** famed for its Delacroix murals and a fine organ, are liable to figure on the tourist's checklist. But St.-Germain itself is a marvelous area to wander around. It's busy, colorful, and cosmopolitan, with an accumulation of "in"cafés, restaurants, and bars among immaculate high-fashion shops and elegant buildings. The cafés **Flore, Aux Deux Magots, Lipp,** and **Bonaparte** on the busy boulevard St.-Germain have all remained distinctly elegant and sophisticated.

The little streets to the north of the boulevard St.-Germain—the rue Jacob, the rue Bonaparte, the rue de Seine, and the rue de Mazarine—are packed with clubs, restaurants, food shops (there's a particularly good food market in the rue de Seine), and art galleries. There's an indefinably Gallic quality about the whole area. It's unmistakably chic despite being slightly shabby; it's crammed full of excellent restaurants; and it's full of unexpected nooks and crannies revealing hidden treasures. One such is in the place Furstemberg, a little square just off the rue Jacob. Here the 19th-century painter Delacroix had his studio, which has been turned into a charming little museum (open daily except Tuesday from 9:45 to 5:15).

Anyone hoping to break away from the beaten path of mass tourism should seriously consider staying in this area—see 6th Arrondissement in the Hotel listings for details. For a combination of charm, character, and convenience—it is, after all, very central—St.-Germain is hard to beat.

The Musée d'Orsay

The newest museum in Paris, the **Musée d'Orsay,** opened early in 1987 and immediately became one of the city's most popular attractions. To reach it from St.-Germain, follow the rue Jacob westward, continue along the rue de l'Université, then turn right towards the river on rue Bellechasse.

The Musée d'Orsay, like so many Parisian museums, is fascinating as a building in its own right. It was built as a rail station in the late 1890s, but had only a short working life. Electrification of the railways created longer trains that wouldn't fit under the great arched roof. The station was saved from demolition in 1978 by being classified as an historical monument, legislation which paved the way for its transformation into a museum to house fine and applied arts from the period 1848–1914.

The huge job of converting the interior was given to an Italian architect, Gae Aulenti, who divided the building into three main areas: the soaring space under the old station roof; the splendid public rooms of the former hotel that run down one side of the complex; and the rooms on the upper floors of the hotel. She created what looks like the bottom half of a De Mille film set, built out of limestone, to fill the area where the tracks used to run. The art on display here is massive, with acres of canvas and tons of stone, while more intimate pieces can be seen in the surrounding maze of small walled areas.

The middle level, partly in the old hotel, is a glorious mixture of paintings, furniture, sculpture, china, and glass, a lot of it Art Nouveau. One of the highlights is part of the original building, the Salle des Fêtes, a faithfully restored Belle Epoque room with crystal swags and mirrors. On the floor above are the Impressionists and other late-1800s artists. There are pictures here known across the world—works by Manet, Monet, Renoir, Degas, Van Gogh, Cézanne, Degas, Toulouse Lautrec, and others. If these are painters who interest you, arrive early in the day and head directly to these rooms. Later in the day, it's almost impossible to get near the works of art you want to see. Up here, too, you can look out across the Seine to the Tuileries garden through the glass face of one of the two great clocks.

There is a rooftop café and a restaurant, but there are always long lines around lunchtime. Indeed, it's almost impossible to get into the restaurant without a reservation. The area around the museum has plenty of quiet places to eat that can take up the overflow.

The museum is open 10:30 to 6, Tuesday, Wednesday, Friday, and Saturday; Sunday, 9 to 6; Thursday, 10:30 to 9:45; closed Monday.

THE MUSÉE RODIN AND THE INVALIDES

Return to the rue Bellechasse when you leave the museum, walk away from the river, cross the boulevard St.-Germain, and then turn right on to the rue de Varenne. You will have been walking through the heart of French bureaucracy, for these streets contain many government offices, among them the Ministry of Education, the Ministry of Industry, and the Ministry of Agriculture.

On the lefthand side of the rue de Varenne, at the very end, is the **Musée Rodin** (also called the Hôtel Biron), nestling in a big garden. This attractive old house was once the home and studio of France's greatest sculptor, some of whose work you will just have seen at the d'Orsay. There is lots more of it here. The rooms are full of pieces at every stage of evolution, as well as his working sketches. You can relax in the gardens, which are especially pretty in late spring and summer. Some of the most important sculptures have been set out under the trees.

The Hôtel Biron is open daily, except Tuesday, 10 to 5:45 (4:30 October through February); half price on Sunday.

Across the road from the Musêe Rodin is the symbolic core of the French obsession with Glory, the tomb of Napoleon and the **Musée de l'Armée** (the Army Museum). The museum is so well planned, and so full of fascinating historical exhibits, that it should grip even those who aren't normally interested in military things. Behind the museum is the great Church of the Dome, the vast structure that guards Napoleon's red porphyry tomb. The setting was designed with an eye to giving the little Emperor the kind of theatrical grandeur in death that he strove for in life. The tomb is sunk into a circular crypt, so that you can look down on it. You can also descend to the level of the crypt for a closer view. Between the huge, domed mausoleum and the museum lies the Church of **St. Louis des Invalides,** hung with tattered flags, captured from France's enemies. There is a *Son et Lumière* show telling the story of the return to Paris of Napoleon's remains from St. Helena, the lonely Atlantic island where the Emperor passed his last unhappy days. It is given twice nightly, once in English and once in French.

The museum is open daily 10 to 5 (to 6, April through September). The tomb may be visited up to 7 all year.

From the place Vauban, behind the Church of the Dome, turn right along avenue de Tourville, then left to reach the southern end of the Champ de Mars, a long orderly park which leads straight back to the Seine and the Eiffel Tower, where your tour began.

Hotels

Finding the right hotel in Paris is easy. The city is full of places to stay in all price categories. Prices are not always low—at the top end of the scale there's practically no limit to how much you can pay—but you will usually get value for money. The French have a real flair for running hotels, and have long since mastered the art of combining comfort and efficiency.

There are some practical points to bear in mind. First, book ahead. Parisian hotels, especially the better ones, tend to be booked up some time in advance, whether by delegates attending one of the many trade fairs or by tourists. You can book through your travel agent or direct with the hotel. Alternatively, try *Hotel Service Paris,* 42 rue le Peletier, 75009 Paris (tel. 42-80-18-53). In the U.S., call them at 800-361-1304 (telex 641 645 F). Second, French hotels charge by the room, not per person, a thoroughly sensible system. Most rooms are doubles. The few single ones left tend to be pokey and on a top floor. Third, a *salle de bain,* whatever your school French may tell you, could be just a shower (if you want a real soaking tub you have to ask for a *baignoire*). Fourth, only the expensive hotels will have air-conditioning, so, if the hotel you choose is on a noisy street, ask for a room *sur cour* (many hotels are built round a courtyard), or away from the street. Fifth, the French, perhaps with memories of the guillotine, often sleep with a torture device like a solid sausage, called a *traversin,* an old-fashioned bolster. If you want a restful night, ask for *oreillers,* pillows.

Apartments can be rented from *Paris-Accueil,* 23 rue de Marignan, 8e (tel. 45-56-20-00). This is not the least expensive renting service in Paris, but the apartments are first class. They also run a apartment exchange scheme with New Yorkers.

We have arranged the following hotels by arrondissement, covering the central ones only.

First Arrondissement

Family Hotel, 35 rue Cambon (tel. 42-61-54-84). A small inexpensive hotel with extremely friendly atmosphere. It can be a real pleasure to stay here. Not all the rooms have bathrooms, however, so book early.

Londres Stockholm, 13 rue St.-Roch (tel. 42-60-15-62). 28 rooms, 26 with bath or shower. Moderately priced, and very conveniently located near the Palais Royal and the Tuileries Gardens.

Normandy, 7 rue de l'Echelle (tel. 42-60-30-21). 120 rooms, all with bath. A comfortable hotel, attractively decorated. There's a good restaurant, plus a relaxing, wood-paneled bar. Excellent location just north of the rue du Rivoli and the Tuileries Gardens. Rates are moderate.

Palais, 2 quai de la Mégisserie (tel. 42-36-98-25). 19 rooms, a few with bath or shower. Not the greatest hotel in the world, but the low rates and the excellent location on the Ile de la Cité, opposite the Sainte-Chapelle, make it a worthwhile bet.

Ritz, 15 pl. Vendôme (tel. 42-60-38-30). 163 rooms and suites. This is one of the top hotels in Paris, indeed in Europe, offering an equal measure of superb old-world charm and service, and every modern facility, with prices to match. It's owned by the same Egyptian family that now own Harrods in London. They have spared no expense in inaugurating a lavish program of restoration and redevelopment. There are two magnificent restaurants, including *L'Espadon,* two small but renowned bars, a pretty courtyard garden, a swimming-pool, and air-conditioning throughout.

SECOND ARRONDISSEMENT

Choiseul-Opéra, 1 rue Daunou (tel. 42-61-70-41). 43 rooms, all with bath or shower. Excellent location behind the Musée Cognac-Jay, on the same street as the celebrated Harry's Bar, and very close to the Opéra. Moderately priced.

Edouard-VII, 39 av. de l'Opéra (tel. 42-61-56-90). 94 rooms, all with bath or shower. Luxurious spot by the Opéra. The restaurant here, the *Delmonico,* is highly recommended.

Opéra d'Antin l'Horset, 18 rue d'Antin (tel. 47-42-13-01). 60 rooms, 52 with shower. This hotel, expensive if not absolutely in the top bracket, is a member of the well-run Horset chain. However, it's the central location, just off the avenue de l'Opéra, that makes it worth trying, especially for shoppers.

Westminster, 13 rue de la Paix (tel. 42-61-57-46). 102 rooms, all with bath or shower. Restaurant, air-conditioning, and splendid location just off the place Vendôme single out this old favorite. It has recently been completely renovated. Prices are high, but justified.

THIRD ARRONDISSEMENT

Marais, 2 bis rue Commines (tel. 48-87-78-27). 38 rooms, all with bath or shower. A small hotel with comfortable rooms. There are also some connecting rooms for parents with children. Very well situated for the Pompidou Center and Le Marais. Rates are moderate.

Fourth Arrondissement

Bretonnerie, 22 rue Ste.-Croix-de-la-Bretonnerie (tel. 48-87-77-63). 31 rooms, all with bath or shower. Charming 17th-century building near the Hôtel de Ville, the Beaubourg, and the Marais. Antiques decorate some of the rooms, and there's a good bar. Prices are moderate.
    Deux-Iles, 59 rue St.-Louis-en-l'Ile (tel. 43-26-13-35). 17 rooms, all with bath or shower. An attractive small hotel on the residential and elegant Ile St.-Louis; located in a fine 17th-century building. There's a bar and a sitting room in the old cellars. All in all, an excellent deal, especially in view of the less than astronomic prices.
    Lutèce, 65 rue St.-Louis-en-l'Ile (tel. 43-26-23-52). 23 rooms, all with bath or shower. A quiet and comfortable hotel in an historic building. Small—some rooms *very* small—and attractive, with reasonable rates. There's a bar, and a number of duplexes.
    Saint-Louis, 75 rue St.-Louis-en-l'Ile (tel. 46-34-04-80). 21 rooms, all with bath or shower. This is an attractive hotel, offering very good value. Tremendous views from the top story. And peace and quiet comes as standard.

Fifth Arrondissement

Avenir, 52 rue Gay-Lussac (tel. 43-54-76-60). 47 rooms, only 6 with bath or shower. A modest hotel with very low prices. On six floors, with no elevator.
    Colbert, 7 rue de l'Hôtel Colbert (tel. 43-25-85-65). 40 rooms, all with bath or shower. Close to the Seine, just opposite Notre Dame. Attractive, if slightly small rooms,

in an 18th-century building. Comfortable. Prices are high.

Esmeralda, 4 rue St.-Julien-le-Pauvre (tel. 43-54-19-20). 19 rooms, 16 with bath or shower. Very pretty 17th-century building by the attractive square Viviani, just opposite Notre Dame, on the Left Bank. The rooms are smallish, but well furnished, and rates moderate.

Grandes Ecoles, 75 rue Cardinal-Lemoine (tel. 43-26-79-23). The countryside in the heart of Paris. This charming little hotel, tucked at the end of a private alleyway, is an old house with trellised roses growing outside and a small colonnaded garden. The bedrooms are small and simple, but just right, and prices low. Book early.

SIXTH ARRONDISSEMENT

L'Abbaye Saint-Germain, 10 rue Cassette (tel. 45-44-38-11). 45 rooms, all with bath or shower. Originally an abbey—with paved garden and pleasant courtyard to prove it—this is a distinctly discriminating spot in the heart of literary St.-Germain. It's fairly expensive, and you must book well in advance—especially for a first-floor courtyard room—but it's very welcoming.

Angleterre, 44 rue Jacob (tel. 42-60-34-72). 31 rooms, all with bath or shower. Still exuding the atmosphere of a plush private house (it was once the home of the British Ambassador), this is a delightful hotel: small, excellently-run, with extremely comfortable if modest rooms, and a pretty courtyard. And all in the heart of St.-Germain. Unbeatable value.

L'Hôtel, 13 rue des Beaux Arts (tel. 43-25-27-22). 27 rooms, all with bath. The simple name disguises a hotel that's far from plain. This is the only super deluxe hotel on the Left Bank, but it's quite unlike anything else in the city. It's very small, very, very chic (Mick Jagger's a regular), and very expensive. If you're lucky you may even get the room where Oscar Wilde died in 1900.

La Louisiane, rue de Seine (tel. 43-29-59-30). Book early; this place fills up with journalists and Italian models. It's a two-star place, so not too expensive, if somewhat self-consciously simple. It was originally a private home, and long famous as the haunt of Hemingway and Sartre. Can be a bit noisy, so ask for the quieter rooms.

Lutétia, 45 blvd. Raspail (tel. 45-44-38-10). 295 rooms, all with bath or shower. Near the Bon Marché department store, with an attractive atmosphere and good, old-fashioned service. Renovated from top to toe in the mid '80s under the eagle eye of fashion designer Sonia Rykiel. She's produced a supremely elegant modern Art Deco palace. Restaurant and bar too. Expensive.

Saints-Péres, 65 rue des Saints-Péres (tel. 45-44-50-00). 37 rooms, 33 with bath or shower. There's everything here you could want: space, style, and silence (especially in rooms that overlook the gardens), plus a touch of modernity. The mezzanine apartments under the rafters are exclusively for newly-weds and have a perfect garden view. Suprisingly low rates.

Vieux Paris, 9 rue Git-le-Coeur (tel. 43-54-41-66). 21 rooms, 14 with bath or shower. On a picturesque street close to the river and the place St.-Michel. Friendly service, low rates, lots of charm, and an old building produce a winning combination.

SEVENTH ARRONDISSEMENT

Pont-Royal, 7 rue Montalembert (tel. 45-44-38-27). 75 rooms, all with bath or shower. Near the new Orsay Museum. Some of the rooms are cramped considering the deluxe prices, but the atmosphere is attractive and welcoming. There's a good bar and restaurant, and air-conditioning.

Résidence Elysées-Maubourg, 35 blvd. de Latour-Maubourg (tel. 45-56-10-78). 30 rooms, all with bath or shower. An older building, extensively modernized in the mid '80s. Though small, it's very comfortable. Close to Les Invalides and the Eiffel Tower.

Varenne, 44 rue de Bourgogne (tel. 45-51-45-55). 24 rooms, all with bath or shower. A peaceful and friendly one-time private mansion, with a pretty little patio. Very good value for the moderate rates.

Verneuil St.-Germain, 8 rue de Verneuil (tel. 42-60-24-16). 26 rooms, all with bath or shower. A cosy modern hotel, with all amenities—plus beams, stylish wallpaper, and fabrics—on a quiet street. The accent here is very much on charm. Prices are low for what's offered.

EIGHTH ARRONDISSEMENT

Bristol, 112 fbg. St.-Honoré (tel. 42-66-91-45). 205 rooms and suites. One of the most elegant—and expensive—hotels in the city. Close to the British Embassy and just a stone's throw from the Elysée Palace, it's in the throbbing heart of chic Paris. Luxury abounds. There's also an excellent restaurant, and a swimming-pool.

Chambiges, 8 rue Chambiges (tel. 47-23-80-49). 30 rooms, 22 with bath or shower. Pleasant and modest little hotel close to the Seine and the avenue Montaigne. There are a few more expensive rooms, but rates are otherwise moderate.

Crillon, 10 pl. de la Concorde (tel. 42-65-24-24). 146 rooms. The grandiose site, with views over the place de la Concorde to the National Assembly, and building have long since made this super deluxe hotel an institution. It's a regular stopping off point for top Americans, and has been since Benjamin Franklin and Thomas Jefferson stayed here when it was a private palace. A thorough renovation in the early '80s has kept it comfortable and ultra smart. It also boasts just about the best hotel restaurant—*Les Ambassadeurs*—in the city.

George V, 31 av. George V (tel. 47-23-54-00). 292 rooms. Located close to the Champs-Elysées, this ultra-fashionable haunt is popular with oil sheiks, movie stars, businessmen, and mere millionaires alike. The bar is almost a club for those who pull the strings that count. Every facility you can think of, and a few more beside.

Lancaster, 7 rue de Berri (tel. 43-59-90-43). 47 rooms, all with bath. Luxury, exclusivity, and impeccable service single out the Lancaster as a quite phenomenally good hotel. The furnishings are magnificent, the restaurant excellent, and there's a charming little garden. The location, just off the Champs Elysées and close to the Arc de Triomphe, is equally desirable.

Roblin, 6 rue Chauveau-Lagarde (tel. 42-65-57-00). 67 rooms, 62 with bath or shower. Well-placed near the Madeleine and good for serious shoppers: The Faubourg St.-Honoré and the big department stores are all close at hand. Good restaurant—*Le Mazagran* (closed August and weekends)—and bar. Fairly expensive, but not bank-breakingly so.

Le Tremoille, 14 rue de la Tremoille (tel. 47-23-34-20). 97 rooms, all with bath or shower. Good service, all modern facilities, and period furnishings. Prices are high, but value is good. Near the Champs-Elysées and the *couture* houses (popular with top models and their escorts).

Restaurants

Food is more than just important to the French. It is a way of life, an art form, an indispensable part of being. In recent years the French Government has officially recognized the Art and Science of French Cuisine, and awarded a sizeable grant for its study, research, promotion, and practice. Figures such as Michel Guérard, Paul Bocuse, the Troisgros brothers, Michel Oliver and his son Raymond, Jean-Claude Bucher, Alain Senderens, and Roger Vergé are more than just household names: They are almost demi-gods.

There is a veritable embarrassment of riches from which to choose, from tiny, neighborhood cafés and bistrots to the plushest temples of gastronomic delight, with just about everything in between: *cuisine bourgeoise, nouvelle cuisine, cuisine regionale,* even, for the desperate, Burger King. If you are after a complete, formal dinner, then *grande cuisine* is the one. If you prefer a lighter touch, yet still with a recognizably traditional twist, try *cuisine bourgeoise*. For an even lighter approach, with pure flavors, freshness, and an imaginative combination of ingredients (but often served in miniscule portions: There's a saying that this style means less on the plate but more on the check), go for *nouvelle cuisine*. *Cuisine regionale* in Paris is similarly excellent, marked by an enormous variety of traditional and specifically regional ingredients, and much ingenuity. There are also countless ethnic restaurants in the city, ranging from Chinese, Vietnamese, Japanese, Russian, and Kosher to Algerian, Moroccan, and Tunisian, with a fair sprinkling of Indian and Indonesian haunts thrown in for good measure.

A word about prices: Parisian restaurants still offer generally good value for money. Catering to such a discriminating clientele, the city's restauranteurs keep prices low and offer value for money or go out of business faster than you can say *Garçon!* Most of the places we recommend here are not, therefore, excessively expensive, though where they are more expensive than the norm we say so (as do we also for the really inexpensive places). But always make a point of checking the menu posted outside before you go in. If you think it unreasonable, go elsewhere. You'll never have trouble finding a substitute: Paris is a city of restaurants. You should also be sure to check the credit card stickers in the window. Don't assume that all the major cards will be accepted, even in the ritziest spots, because they won't.

If you are watching your dollars carefully, then be sure to check out the set menus (*menu* in French—an *à la carte* menu is a different animal). Nearly all restaurants have several at different prices. The ones with especially interesting cuisine may have a gourmet *menu*. This will allow you to taste several of the chef's specialties at much less than if you had ordered them as separate dishes.

A final word of warning: Parisian restaurants have very variable opening times. A good many close for all or part of July and (especially) August. Similarly, a great many close on weekends, particularly Sundays and public holidays. Always check before turning up.

No guide could ever do justice to the restaurants of Paris. Even the most comprehensive can present no more than the tip of the iceberg. The restaurants listed here, arranged by arrondissement, represent a mélange of the tried and the tested and the novel. But for every one we recommend there are probably another 20 just as good. Never be afraid to experiment. *Bon Appétit!*

First Arrondissement

L'Absinthe, 24 place du Marché St.-Honoré (tel. 42-60-02-45). Friendly service in this chic little restaurant, close to place Vendôme and the avenue de l'Opéra. The cooking is mostly "new," with delectably fresh ingredients. Attractive decor with Art Nouveau bits and pieces. Closed Saturday for lunch, and Sunday.

Gérard Besson, 5 rue de Coq-Heron (tel. 42-33-14-74). Gérard Besson and Martine and Alain Delaveyne will welcome you to their English pub-like restaurant in the heart of the old Les Halles quarter. Excellent game, wild mushrooms, and deliciously-prepared fish, plus a cozy, low-key ambience. Closed three weeks in July, one week for Christmas, and Saturday and Sunday.

L'Escargot Montorgueil, 38 rue Montorgueil (tel. 42-36-83-51). In the middle of what used to be Les Halles food market. Opened in the 1830s and still going strong, with delightful 19th-century decor of mirrors and traditional wall sofas. A chic clientele. Snails, of course, and many other good dishes. Closed May 1, and one week around August 15.

Bistro de la Gare, 30 rue St.-Denis (tel. 42-60-84-92). One of four similar restaurants run by Michel Oliver. Good, reliable food, with a special speedy service for theater-goers, is the order of the day. The restaurant open every day of the year, with last orders at around midnight.

Gourmet's, 26 pl. Dauphine (tel. 43-26-72-92). Located in a pretty square behind the Law Courts and the Ste.-Chapelle on the Ile de la Cité, this is a curious but excellent French/Scandinavian *nouvelle cuisine* restaurant, enjoying a richly deserved success. Prices are high, but the decor is stylish and the food excellent. And there are also 130 wines to choose from. Reservations are essential. Closed Monday.

Le Grand Véfour, 17 rue de Beaujolais (tel. 42-96-56-27). The fact that two weeks is the minimum time you have to book ahead to get in here, and even then there's no guarantee of success, underlines only too clearly that this is one of the great gastronomic experiences Paris has to offer. Excellent food, superb service. Need we say more?

Le Noailles, 6 rue du 29 Juillet (tel. 42-96-57-11). Actually the restaurant of the Hotel St.-James and Albany. Large and sophisticated, ideal both for low-profile business lunches and couples who want to be left to themselves. The courtyard comes into its own in the summer, and makes a delightful spot for outdoor dining. *Nouvelle* and *regionale cuisine,* and a good value set *menu,* though prices are otherwise quite high.

Mercure Galant, 15 rue des Petits Champs (tel. 42-97-53-85). A charmingly elegant Parisian house with fine *fin de siécle* decor. It's very popular. Prices can be high except for the good value *menu.* Often very busy, so book ahead. Try the *terrine Ferranti,* the *feuilleté de langoustines,* and the delicious desserts. Owners Pierre Ferranti and Jean-Marie Bracco will make sure you have a magnificent evening. Closed July, over Christmas period, and weekends.

Chez Pauline, 5 rue Villedo (tel. 42-96-20-70). Not far from the Palais Royal, between the rue de Richelieu and the rue St.-Anne, this warm, friendly bistrot offers good service and excellent traditional food, much of it suprisingly light, in pleasant surroundings. Closed most of July, Saturday lunch April through September, all Saturdays for dinner, Sunday.

Pharamond, 24 rue de la Grande Truanderie (tel. 42-33-06-72). In the heart of Les Halles, with beautiful and original turn-of-the-century decor. Specializes in dishes from Normandy. Closed Sunday, Monday for lunch, and July.

Rôtisserie-Rivoli, Hotel Inter-Continental, 3 rue de Castiglione (tel. 42-60-37-80). Although part of a luxury hotel, the Rôtisserie-Rivoli offers excellent value for money. Try the *menu:* it has two *plats du jour.* Chef Jean-Jacques Barbier makes a point of insisting on high quality and copious portions. There's an Italian-style patio for outdoor dining in the summer.

Willi's Wine Bar, 13 rue des Petits Champs (tel. 42-61-05-09). A little bit of England flavored with Parisian panache. Impeccably-mannered young ladies of the very best breeding serve you good quality Anglo-French food, and wine by the glass. It's always crowded. Open from 11 A.M. to 11 P.M. Closed Sundays and public holidays.

SECOND ARRONDISSEMENT

L'Amanguier, 110 rue de Richelieu (tel. 42-96-37-39). Like a summer's day in the country. The captivating green-and-white decor, with parasols and garden chairs, and the short but imaginative menu, with extremely reasonable prices, make this a real find. The desserts are particularly good. Near the Bourse and quite close to the Opéra. Open to 11:30 P.M. Closed May 1.

Bistrot du Fort, 20 passage des Panoramas (tel. 45-08-89-19). This is a most eccentric place. The food is not that special, though it's very inexpensive. But then it's not the food you come for. Patron Pierre Monneret, a household name as a motorbike racer many years ago, as the cuttings, photos, medals, and cups make clear, presents a floor show with a difference at nine every evening. He serenades his clientele with ballads of his days on the motorbike circuits of the world before treating them to films of his many victories. A laugh a minute. Open till late.

Le Petit Coin de la Bourse, 16 rue Feydeau (tel. 45-08-00-08). Another businessman's restaurant, with mouthwatering food at excellent prices. Lunch reservations essential. Try *Symphonie de poisson marinés* or *Saumon sauvage à l'oseille*. And don't miss the exquisite *Tarte aux pommes:* it's always made specially, so you have to order it more or less as you arrive. Closed weekends.

Pierre à la Fontaine Gaillon, pl. Gaillon (tel. 42-65-87-04). A delightful restaurant, with excellent and friendly service. There's a leafy enclosed terrace in the summer. The food is traditional for the most part, and first class. This is another good place to come after the opera. Closed August, Saturday for lunch, and Sunday.

Pile ou Face, 52 bis rue Notre Dame des Victoires (tel. 42-33-64-33). Tiny upstairs diningroom, popular at lunchtime with stockbrokers from the nearby Bourse, and with couples seeking romance in the evening. Mostly *nouvelle cuisine*. Prices are moderate. Closed weekends and August.

THIRD ARRONDISSEMENT

L'Ambassade d'Auvergne, 22 rue du Grenier-St.-Lazar (tel. 42-72-31-22). Just around the corner from Nicholas Flamel's ancient house is a restaurant that deserves a special mention. It's run by the Petrucci family, and graced by an Auvergnat cook by the name of Jean Yves Delourme. He offers *Mourtayrol*, a *pot-au-feu* from the Auvergne the likes of which you will never have tasted before; *Estofinado*, a mouth-watering fish dish; and a sensational tripe, spinach, and apple concoction that answers to the name of *Tripous à l'Estragon pommes fondantes*. Prices are high, but well worth it. Closed Sunday.

Janou, 2 rue Roger-Verlomme (tel. 42-72-28-41). An adorable little terrace a short walk from the Marais, presided over by the beautiful Janou. She offers her variation of gazpacho, *sauté d'agneau à la menthe*. Very friendly. Closed Saturday and Sunday.

Le Mille Feuilles, 2 rue Rambuteau (tel. 42-78-32-93). Pierre Brinon decorates his walls with white tissue on blue, producing an agreeably romantic little spot. Try the *Koulibiac de saumon* and the *Salade de confit*. Rates are reasonable, especially for the weekend brunch.

Daniel Tuboeuf, 26 rue de Montmorency (tel. 42-72-31-04). Daniel Tuboeuf worked with Gérard Pangaud, the *nouvelle cuisine* wizard, and at Pierre Traiteur, before opening this little gem of a bistrot in the heart of the Marais. Good fish, a *foie gras de canard* that's absolutely out of this world, and sea bass terrine with sea urchin sauce. Closed Saturday and Sunday, and end-July to early-September.

Fourth Arrondissement

La Colombe, 4 rue de la Colombe (tel. 46-33-37-08). Tucked away in a little sidestreet near Notre Dame, this is believed to be the oldest bistrot in the city. No attempt has been made to update either the decor or the cuisine, so those in search of a Paris that has all but disappeared elsewhere should make a visit here a priority. Open-air dining beneath a romantic vine trellis to the strains of 18th-century music just makes the whole thing all the more wonderful. Service can be a bit slapdash, however. Open till late. Closed Sunday, Monday for lunch, and most of August.

Courrier Sud, 19 rue Francois-Miron (tel. 42-78-64-54). Spruce and rather discreet little bistrot in the Marais that's ideal for *liaisons dangereuses* (though of course you don't *have* to be having an affair to come here). The food's simple, and excellently cooked in the traditional bistrot style. Prices are low for what's offered, especially the Sunday brunch. Open late.

Le Domarais, 53 bis rue des Francs-Bourgeois (tel. 42-74-54-17). From the outside this place looks as though it's part of the Banque Credit Municipal de Commerce. But head through the courtyard and you step into a richly luxurious salon, with glass dome, deeply-lacquered wood, gold leaf, plants, and classical statutes. The food is every bit as good as the astounding decor, with an equal mixture of *nouvelle* and *bourgeois cuisine*. Excellent wines. Closed weekends, August, and Christmas.

Quai des Ormes, 72 quai de l'Hôtel de Ville (tel. 42-74-72-22). A rather chic restaurant, very well located by the Seine. Serves *nouvelle cuisine*, and has good value *menus* for lunch. Closed weekends and August.

La Rose Daisy, 54 rue des Rosiers (tel. 42-78-23-09). What a find! Magnificent kosher food in a sprucely modern restaurant in the heart of the Marais, the whole presided over by the one and only Rav Rottenburg. Open late.

FIFTH ARRONDISSEMENT

Atelier Maître Albert, 1–5 rue Maître Albert (tel. 26-33-13-78). This is seriously solid food, with the added benefit of a roaring log fire in the winter and air-conditioning in the summer. The menu's simple, but ultra-reliable. Open late. Closed weekends and public holidays.

Le Balzar, 49 rue des Ecole (tel. 43-54-13-67). A genuine *brasserie,* complete with waiters in long white aprons and worthily traditional food. Low prices and terrific atmosphere. *Very* busy at lunch. Closed Tuesday, and August.

Dodin Bouffant, 25 rue Frederic-Sauton (tel. 43-25-25-14). One of the finest—and most fashionable—restaurants in Paris. Inspired *nouvelle cuisine,* with the emphasis on freshness and lightness. Great salt-water tanks wait in the cellars below, alive with oysters, lobsters, and fish of every description. Exquisite desserts, wines fit for a king, outdoor dining, and remarkably reasonable prices complete the picture, but reserve well ahead. Closed Sunday.

Perraudin, 157 rue St. Jacques (tel. 46-33-15-75). Classical small bistrot near the Sorbonne and the Panthéon; a rendezvous for poets, students, and professors. Traditional French cooking and atmosphere. Very reasonable *menus,* with specialties including quail with cabbage and bacon, onion soup, and *gratin dauphinois.* On the corner of rue St. Jacques and rue Soufflot.

La Tour d'Argent, 15 quai de la Tournelle (tel. 43-54-23-31). This is probably the most expensive restaurant in Paris. Certainly it's the most famous. You pay for a table overlooking Notre Dame (illuminated at night), perfect service that ministers to your every whim, and the highest of *haute cuisine.* Mind you, people do say the Tour d'Argent is not what it used to be, at least as far as the food is concerned. But it remains a staggering experience, *and* they have a fixed priced *menu* at lunch that works out at about half the price of eating *à la carte.*

SIXTH ARRONDISSEMENT

B.D. 36, 36 rue Gregoire-de-Tours (tel. 46-34-20-26). What a strange place! Part art gallery, part restaurant, with videos filling the spaces in between, this is *the* artsy place to head for at the moment, but not before 11 P.M. You won't regret a moment of your visit, or a mouthful of your meal.

Le Cabécou, 151 rue de Vaurigard (tel. 47-34-72-46). A small restaurant offering dishes of the highest quality from Quercy, a region next to the Dordogne. Duck, goose, and truffles abound; try the *confit de canard* or *d'oie, magret de canard,* or *gateaux de noix*. There's only about a dozen dishes, but they're all excellent.

Aux Charpentiers, 10 rue Mabillon (tel. 43-26-30-05). Classic Parisian bistrot, unpretentious and altogether delightful. Used to be the headquarters of the Carpenters' Guild. Plain, straightforward, homey dishes, that are very reasonably priced. Closed Sunday, and New Year.

Les Classiques, 22 passage Dauphine (tel. 46-34-00-40). Post-modernism rules supreme here in the heart of St.-Germain—the name should be taken literally. Marble tables, bas-reliefs of bathing women, and carefully marbled walls combine to produce an unmistakably classical ambience. It's all very chic. The food is *nouvelle cuisine* (of course). Prices are fairly low, however. And there's a good weekend brunch.

Le Procope, 13 rue de l'Ancienne Comédie (tel. 43-26-99-20). A large, bustling, crowded café-restaurant, this place goes way back. La Fontaine, Voltaire, Rousseau, Benjamin Franklin, Napoleon, and Balzac all knew it. It's unbeatable for warmth and atmosphere, but the food's not the main reason for coming. Open to 1:30, closed July.

Petit St-Benoît, 4 rue St-Benoît (no telephone reservations). This is a wonderful place. Small, amazingly inexpensive, always crowded, very simple—the true heart of St.-Germain beats inside its plain walls. Likely as not you'll find yourself sharing a table, but you can be sure it'll be with a kindred spirit. Closed weekends, and mid-July to mid-August.

Le Petit Zinc, 25 rue de Buci (tel. 43-54-79-34). An old favorite—ever popular, ever crowded, with tables outside in summer. In common with many Parisian restaurants, it serves excellent oysters. Open till 3 A.M.

Restaurant des Saints-Pères, blvd. St.-Germain (tel. 45-48-56-85). An old favorite, if a little overpriced these days. But you'll love the traditional marble counter, the bentwood hatstand, the little dishes of *crudités* carefully arranged in symphonies of colors, the baskets of walnuts in season, and the glass panels. This, in other words, is the genuine article: a Parisian bistrot in all its glory. Go soon. There aren't many left, and the grumpy waitresses in their black dresses can't go on forever. Sidewalk tables in the summer. Closed Wednesday, Thursday, and mid-August to mid-September.

SEVENTH ARRONDISSEMENT

Chez des Anges, 54 blvd. de Latour-Maubourg (tel. 47-05-89-86). A spacious and comfortable spot near Les Invalides, offering a judicious mixture of *nouvelle* and classical cooking, the latter mostly from Burgundy. Expensive, but generally good to know. Closed Sunday for dinner and Monday.

La Fontaine de Mars, 129 rue St.-Dominique (tel. 47-05-46-44). Typically French little restaurant near the Eiffel Tower. It's very much a no-frills place, but its straightforward home cooking has long been popular with the locals in this chic area. You can eat outside in the summer by a fountain in the little square. Prices are definitely low for what's offered. Closed Saturday for dinner, Sunday, and August.

Chez Françoise, Invalides Air Terminal (tel. 47-05-

49-03). Good newish cuisine and an impressive wine list constitute the major attractions in this old-style Parisian haunt. Despite the uninspiring location, it's very popular with diplomats and politicians from the nearby National Assembly. Closed Sunday for dinner, Monday, and August.

Jules Verne, Entrance by Pilier Sud. Eiffel Tower (tel. 45-55-61-44). Opened only in 1985, this restaurant on the second story of the Eiffel Tower is very much more than just a gimmick. The setting is, of course, incomparable, but it's the food that rules supreme here. Prices are very high and reservations hard to come by, but if you can get in it's not an experience you'll forget quickly—this is really a view to dine by.

La Petite Chaise, 36 rue de Grenelle (tel. 42-22-13-35). One of the oldest restaurants in Paris, and still always full. Charming, slightly shabby and traditional atmosphere. The cooking is traditional, too, and excellent value. Open every day.

Au Quai d'Orsay, 49 quai d'Orsay (tel. 45-51-58-58). This pleasing spot has long been fashionable, and never seems to lose its popularity. Good value traditional dishes, very carefully cooked, with some highly imaginative touches; and all at moderate prices. Closed Sunday, and August.

EIGHTH ARRONDISSEMENT

Alsace, 39 av. des Champs Elysées (tel. 43-59-44-24). Chic brasserie serving *choucroute,* beautifully fresh seafood, and superb fruit tarts, as well as the delicious light wines for which Alsace is famous. Has a shop selling regional delicacies next door. Open all day and all night.

Lucas-Carton-Alain Senderens, pl. de la Madeleine (tel. 42-65-22-90). The Lucas-Carton has long been famed for its magnificent Belle Epoque *art nouveau* decor. Now, however, it also boasts a resident genius in the kitchens, Alain Senderens, the master of *nouvelle cuisine* at its subtle best. This is a place for true afficionados. Very expensive. Closed weekends, most of August, and Christmas.

Maxim's, 3 rue Royale (tel. 42-65-27-94). Another Belle Epoque landmark. This ultra-chic restaurant is today a part of couturier Pierre Cardin's empire, under whose auspices it has been revitalized from top to toe. Prices are very high, but more moderate meals are served on the second floor, and there's also a fixed-priced after-theater supper served from 11 P.M. Open to 1 A.M., closed Sunday.

Taillevent, 15 rue Lamennais (tel. 45-61-12-90). If you reserve several months in advance for dinner, and several weeks in adance for lunch, there's a fighting chance you might get a table here. Is this the best restaurant in Paris? Probably, but who can say for sure? Superb *nouvelle cuisine,* perfect service, exquisite surroundings, a truly phenomenal wine list. What more could you want? Closed weekends, one week in February and August, and public holidays.

NINTH ARRONDISSEMENT

Casa Miguel, rue St.-Georges (no telephone reservations). It might almost be worth coming to Paris simply to eat here. Not because it's a temple of gastronomic delights but because it's probably the least expensive restaurant in Europe, certainly in Paris (and has an entry in the Guinness Book of Records to prove it). The price is an astounding five francs, for which you get a three-course meal *with* wine. The menu is naturally somewhat modest, but the delightfully simple decor and genuine bonhomie of the patroness—she's been running the place since 1949—make this somewhere not to be missed. Open 12–1 and 7–8. Get here at least 30 minutes before they open.

Eleventh Arrondissement

Chez Philippe, (Auberge Pyrenées-Cevennes), 106 rue de la Folie-Méricourt (tel. 43-57-33-78). Old café with exquisite food from the southwest of France. Last orders at 10:30 P.M. Closed Saturday, Sunday, and August.

Fifteenth Arrondissement

La Maison Blanche, 82 blvd. Lefebvre (tel. 48-28-38-83). Very plain decor, and a simple and short menu add up to some of the best-value eating in Paris. Closed Saturday for lunch, all day Sunday, Monday, and two weeks in September.

Seventeenth Arrondissement

La Toque, 16 rue de Tocqueville (tel. 42-27-97-75). Tiny but comfortable bistrot serving excellent food (chef worked with Michel Guérard). Good value *menu*. Closed Saturday, Sunday, August, and Christmas.

Cafés and Bars

Cafés are a central part of the Parisian scene, both by day and by night. People-watching from a sidewalk café is one of the eternal delights of this city, one that's hard to tire of. There are hundreds—maybe thousands—of cafés all over Paris, ranging from the chic spots on the Champs Elysées and the intellectual haunts in Saint-Germain and Montparnasse to the simple neighborhood corner cafés where the locals gather to gossip, play cards, have a bite to eat, and watch T.V.

Prices vary greatly. The smart places can be suprisingly expensive. Elsewhere, prices are generally very low. But you can linger for as long as you want over your coffee or drink, so even the most expensive places won't break the bank. Prices are naturally lower if you stand at the bar rather than have a waiter or waitress serve you at a table. But don't order from the bar and then move to a table. The manager will certainly come over and rebuke you.

Café de la Paix, 12 blvd. des Capucines, 9e. Just by the Opéra and long popular with wealthy foreign tourists. Try also the restaurant here, the *Opéra*.

La Coupole, 102 blvd. du Montparnasse, 14e. This

is one of the great Parisian cafés, a little expensive these days, but the real thing nonetheless. Times have changed, of course, since the days when Joyce, Hemingway, Pound, Cocteau, et al, used to come here, but this substantial café-brasserie is still well worth a visit. Bar is open 12–1:30 P.M. and 6–1:30 A.M..

Deux Magots, 179 blvd. St.-Germain, 6e. Not the intellectuals' mecca it was in the heyday of existentialism when Sartre and Co. virtually lived here, but still fashionable, and probably the best place for people-watching. You even get street entertainment thrown in every once in a while: fire-eaters, acrobats, mimes, and the like.

Le Dôme, 108 blvd. du Montparnasse, 14e. This is the other great Montparnasse café. The new decor—a peculiar species of fake *art nouveau*—is not entirely successful, but for a taste of café-society Le Dôme is still one of *the* places to head for.

Le Flore, 172 blvd. St.-Germain, 6e. Next door to the Deux Magots, though it doesn't share its unbeatable corner location. Upstairs is a traditional gay meeting place, but the sidewalk tables are for all comers. It changed hands a few years back, but the new owners have had to guarantee to leave it just as it's always been.

Fouquet's, 99 av. des Champs-Elysées, 8e. Very chic and predictably expensive. This is a place to be seen. There's a good bar, too. Open 8 A.M. till 2 the following morning.

Lipp, 151 blvd. St.-Germain, 6e. Officially a brasserie—and as such it's a regular institution, and favorite haunt of politicos, writers, and film folk—this is still a good place to come for just a coffee or aperitif.

Le Sélect, 99 blvd. du Montparnasse, 6e. Much of the atmosphere of old Montparnasse lingers on here, despite the rebuilding that has done so much to transform the area. Open late.

BARS

With cafés so ubiquitous, Paris has few regular bars. After all, if you can always get a drink in a café, who needs a bar? But there's a fair sprinkling nonetheless (many confusingly called cafés). Among the more popular are:

Le Bar, 38 rue de Conde, 6e. There's no problem trying to figure out if this place is a bar or a café. This is one of the classic spots, and enduringly popular. It's always had a sophisticated clientele, especially from 2 in the morning, when it's just beginning to hit its stride.

Les Bouchons, 19 rue des Halles, 1er. Piano bar with entertainment from 11 P.M. until 2 A.M. Try the first-floor restaurant.

La Calavados, 40 av. Pierre-Ier-de-Serbie, 8e. A favorite haunt of the smart drinking set. This, too, is very much an after-hours bar; not surprisingly, seeing as it's open 24 hours a day.

City Rock Café, 13 rue de Berri, 8e. Open till 4 A.M., this place is the half-brother of the Hard Rocks in London and New York. It's all here ... a Cadillac that belonged to Elvis, a dress that belonged to Marilyn Monroe, one of Indiana Jones' shirts. There are regular gigs, too; past stars have included Michel Axel, Duran Duran, and Ringo. Hamburgers and banana splits are very much the order of the day.

La Closerie des Lilas, 171 blvd. du Montparnasse, 6e. Voices have been raised claiming that this firmly artistic and literary spot is overrated these days, a shadow of its former self. But it's still going strong, and very popular for a lateish drink. Prices are high though. Open 10:30 A.M.–2:20 A.M.

Harry's Bar, 5 rue Daunou, 2e. Opened originally in 1911, Harry's Bar has never looked back. The Hemingway era may be long gone now, but Harry's Bar goes on. It's always had an American slant, and it stays open year-round till 4 A.M.

Magnétic-Terrace, 12 rue de la Cossonnerie, 1er. This place could equally well qualify as a café, or even a restaurant. But, leaving aside the restaurant and the *salon du thé* on the second floor, the Californian video piano-bar on the first floor is what attracts most. Service in short shorts, an excellent pianist, and the Magnétic cocktails to pulverize you.

Toit de Paris, Hilton hotel, 18 av. de Suffren, 15e. All the big hotels have bars; this is just one among many. The view's pretty good, and you can dance as well as drink.

WINE BARS

As a general rule, the French eat their main meal at lunch. So it can be difficult to find a place for a light lunch if you're not in the mood for just a sandwich or other café food. But over the last few years it's become fashionable among the city's well-heeled younger set to go to wine bars for a glass of wine and a tasty light meal of pâté, cold cuts, or cheese.

Wine bars of this type are mushrooming throughout the city now, mostly full of Yuppies and other chic types, plus a sprinkling of old timers who lived in the district for years. They should not, however, be confused with the old-style *bistrots à vin*. These are principally dives for hardened local drinkers, and rarely offer much in the way of food.

The new wine bars don't stay open late, however, so don't count on them for an evening meal. Few are open at weekends.

Le Café des Sportifs, rue Pierre Lescot, 1er. Not quite what you might think. This place represents the comeback of the *bistrot à vin,* but very much for connoisseurs. Good red wine by the glass, lots of French jokes—a mixed blessing this—and opera sing-songs.

Blue Fox, 25 rue Royale, 8e. In the Cité Berryer. Run by Steven Spurrier, who also presides over the Moulin du Village and the Académie du Vin.

L'Ecluse, 15 quai des Grands-Augustins, 6e. Once a typical Left-Bank cabaret, today this is a slick wine bar with converted gas lamps, *art nouveau* posters, and a distinctly up-market clientele. It's been such a success that it's spawned a mini-chain all over the city, even in chic Neuilly. You'll find the others at: rue Mondétour, 1er; rue du Pont-de-Lodi, 6e; 15 pl. de la Madeleine, 8e; 64 rue du François-1er; 8e; 2 rue du Général Bertier, Neuilly. All are open late.

Le Petit Bacchus, 13 rue du Cherche-Midi, 6e. Wine to go as well as to drink here. Closes at 7:15 P.M.

La Tartine, 24 rue du Rivoli, 4e. Typical Parisian spot, with a regular clientele, a good range of wines, and a friendly atmosphere. Open till around 10 P.M.

JUICE BARS

Juice bars are newcomers to Paris. They're rapidly catching on among the younger generation, who more alert to health-food fads than their elders. The majority of these pleasantly casual places are near the place St.-Michel, with several of them right by the Seine. They're good for a quick break between sightseeing visits, and many also serve good homemade ice cream and milkshakes.

L'Afruitdisiaque, 3 rue du Bourg-Tibourg, 4e. Magnificent ice cream near the Beaubourg. Open all week till 2 A.M. There's also a branch at 5 rue du Cygne, 1er, just by Les Halles.

Le Paradis du Fruit, 28bis rue Louis-le-Grand 2e; and 17 quai des Grands-Augustins, 6e. Salads and tasty pâtisseries. Both open till 2 A.M.

La Passion du Fruit, 71 quai de la Tournelle, 5e. Opposite the Ile St.-Louis and handy for Notre Dame. Open till 2 A.M., but closed afternoons.

Nightlife

Paris has successfully sustained its reputation as one of the great nightlife capitals of the world. And of no area of the multi-faceted world of nightlife is this more true than the great revues and shows. Images of the Can-Can, the Folies-Bergère, the Moulin Rouge, Mistinguett, Maurice Chevalier, Josephine Baker, and the Bluebell Girls have proved amazingly durable. And indeed a great many of the larger shows are extremely good: professional, lavish, slick, and spectacular. But they're not inexpensive, and you'll find you're "expected" to drink champagne. Still, they're packing 'em in night after night, so reserve several days ahead if you want to be sure of getting a decent table. But don't be disappointed if your fellow guests are all tourists. The Japanese in particular have a weakness for Parisian nightlife.

All the revues feature semi-nude bodies as shiny and innocuous as Playboy centerfolds. If your tastes run to something a little rawer, head for the rue St.-Denis, the traditional red-light district. But avoid Pigalle, up by Montmartre. It's as sordid as they come these days.

Shows

Alcazar de Paris, 62 rue Mazarine, 6e (tel. 43-29-02-20). Well-known spot in St.-Germain. Loud and bitchy transvestite revues are the specialty, so it helps if you know the odd French insult.

Don Camilo, 10 rue des Sts.-Pères, 7e (tel. 42-60-20-31). An old favorite. Elegant and sophisticated cabaret show, and excellent food. Prices are more reasonable than most.

Le Caveau des Oubliettes, 1 rue St.-Julien-le-Pauvre, 5e (tel. 43-54-94-97). This famous medieval cellar, complete with fake decor and costumed waiters, seems to have been going for ever. But for nostalgia and kitsch it's unbeatable. Lots of Piaf.

Crazy Horse Saloon, 12 av. George-V, 8e (tel. 47-23-32-32). This claims to be the world's top nude show. If popularity is anything to go by, it's hard to disagree. But the whole thing is distinctly sanitized and slick. Shows nightly at 9:25 and 11:45, plus one at 1 A.M. on Fri. and Sat.

Chez Félix, 23 rue Mouffetard, 5e (tel. 47-07-68-78). Located in the picturesque Contrescarpe area. Have just a drink, or go the whole hog and have a candle-lit dinner. There's live Brazilian music and dancing in the atmospheric cellars, and a floor show upstairs. Atmospheric and light-hearted.

Folies-Bergére, 32 rue Richer, 9e (tel. 32-46-77-11). Strictly a theater, where your ticket buys you a seat for the show rather than dinner or a drink. It's still probably the best-known name, with extravagant sets, showy costumes, elaborate sound effects, and spectacular semi-nude dancers, but the glorious days of Chevalier and Mistinguett have long since faded. Still, a certain glamor lingers on.

Le Lapin Agile, 22 rue des Saules, 18e (tel. 46-06-85-87). Le Lapin Agile won its reputation in the early years of the century when Montmartre's artist colony caroused their nights away here. But it's still fun, even if strictly run for the benefit of tourists now. The wooden tables, lively atmosphere, and the show—mostly old French songs, with a handful of newer ones—remain a winning combination.

Lido, 116 av. des Champs-Elysées, 8e (tel. 45-63-11-61). This is *the* place for spectacular entertainment on the grand scale. Dazzling technical trickery, enormous sets, phenomenal costumes, computerized choreography, and the Bluebell Girls add up to the most lavish show of its kind in Paris. The food is adequate, or worse, but the show's the thing. Dinner-dance at 8, shows at 10:30 and 12:30.

Michou, 80 rue des Martyrs, 18e (tel. 46–06–16–04). Great show, with dinner, every evening. You must book well in advance. Close to Montmartre.

Milliardaire, 68 rue Pierre-Charron, 8e (tel. 42-25-25-17). Once you've been to the Crazy Horse, this is the place to come to see a classy strip (Le Milliardaire used to be known as Le Sexy, and for good reasons). Not much has changed. There's a special late show at 2 A.M.

Moulin Rouge, pl. Blanche, 19e (tel. 46-06-00-19). Still cashing in on the most famous name from Montmartre's heyday, and still specializing in the one and only Can-Can. It's owned and run by the same people as the Lido, so it's very professional if slightly less expensive than its stable-mate. Dinner-dance at 8, shows at 10 and 12.

Le Paradis Latin, 28 rue du Cardinal-Lemoine, 5e (tel. 43-25-28-28). Lively and crowded, with amazing architecture. The shows regularly attract big names, but are otherwise a bit faded at the edges now. Dinner and show at 8, and "champagne revue" at 10 and 12.

CLUBS

Private clubs in Paris are both extremely expensive—a bottle of whiskey has been known to sell for 1,000 frs.—and notoriously difficult to get into. "Club" is a misnomer really, though. Calling a place a club is principally just an excuse to keep out anyone whose face doesn't fit. The best *entrée* is, inevitably, knowing the right people. Failing that, do what you can to look interesting, desirable, chic, and glamorous. And if you still can't get in, never mind. Paris has a great deal more to offer.

L'Atmosphere, 40 rue du Colisee, 8e (tel. 42-25-11-68). Very expensive, very exclusive, and much loved by the super-rich-playboy-beautiful-people-celebrity set.

Castel's, 15 rue Princesse, 6e (tel. 43-26-90-22). If you can get into this place it's a real experience. Members only, but if you happen to be Bianca Jagger there's a chance they might let you in on a quiet night. The prettiest women, the smartest names—you name it, they're all here. Excellent bar and restaurant, good music, videos, discos, the lot.

Régine's, 49 rue Ponthieu, 8e (tel. 43-59-21-60). Régine's may be a teeny bit passé now, but it's still pretty luxurious and chic. Excellent food, and jet-setters of all types.

Le Soixante-Dix-Huit, 78 Champs-Elysées, 8e (tel. 43-59-09-99). It may not be as trendy as it was, but the trapeze artists, the underground pool, the light shows, and stock-exchange reports are all still very much in evidence.

Discos

Paris is packed with discos of every description these days. Some are stylish, some are merely tawdry. Most are in between. Unfortunately, keeping track of them is next to impossible. New ones open and close seemingly overnight. Others change their names every few months, though their decor and ambience frequently weather the changes. Those listed here have proved fairly durable, but don't be surprised if they've changed names, moved premises, folded, or disappeared from the face of the earth by the time you read this.

Most open around 10 or 10:30 and stay on the boil till dawn. Some are closed on Mondays, but a fair number are also open on Sunday afternoons. A few will let in girls free during the week or at other quiet spells.

L'Acid Rendezvous, 33 rue Dauphine, 6e (tel. 43-25-66-33). Worth trying to track down for a night of bliss à la '60s. There's another one—*Acid Rendezvous au Baldi*—at 105 rue Faubourg du Temple, 4e (tel. 42-02-20-52).

Adison Square Gardel, 23 rue du Commandant-Mouchotte, 14e (tel. 43-21-54-58). Rather a respectable clientele here, and a good place for dancing. *Thé dansants* on Monday, Tuesday, and Friday at 4 P.M., plus the occasional "pancake evening" add up to a rather quaint picture.

Les Bains, 7 rue du Bourg-l'Abee, 3e (tel. 48-87-01-80). Originally a public bath house, this subsequently became a serious haunt for New Wave devotees. Today, with a swimming pool much in evidence, and after a great deal of renovation, it's among the city's most popular spots. Very trendy.

Le Gibus, 18 Faubourg du Temple, 10e (tel. 47-00-78-80). Here today and gone tomorrow. It's very "in" at the moment, but may be empty in a few months. There's a distinctly cosmopolitan feel. Anything goes.

La Main Jaune, pl. de la Porte Champerret, 17e. A good place to meet the young Parisians, and to dance on roller skates.

Le Palace, 8 rue du Faubourg-Montmartre, 9e (tel. 42-46-10-87). It all goes on here. There are gay nights, Black nights, drag nights, even *thé dansants.*

Whisky à Gogo, 57 rue du Seine, 6e (tel. 46-33-74-99). A long-time favorite, still popular with the Left Bank crowd. Special psychedelic nights from time to time add spice.

Music, Movies, and Theaters

For details on how to find out what's playing in Paris, see "What's On" in *Paris Briefing*.

MUSIC

JAZZ. The French take jazz seriously and Paris is one of the great jazz cities of the world, with several specialist record shops and an array of clubs. Every type of jazz is available, from the stolidly traditional through classic bebop to jazz-rock and, increasingly, South American and African offshoots.

For precise details of who's on when, see either of the excellent specialist magazines, *Jazz Hot* or *Jazz Magazine*, and listen to the jazz programs on France Musique. Remember that nothing gets going until 10 or 11 P.M., credit cards are almost never accepted, and, although prices are generally reasonable, they vary according to the attraction.

Le Caméléon, 57 rue St.-André-des-Arts, 5e (tel.

43-26-64-40). There was a time when you could be sure of an enthusiastic crowd in this dark record bar, with its downstairs cellar for live music and dancing. It's quieter these days, though the choice of records is still discriminating. Decent range of beers and whiskies, but no exotic cocktails. Inexpensive.

Le Caveau de la Huchette, 5 rue de la Huchette, 5e (tel. 43-26-65-05). Large stone cellar in student (and tourist) quarter. An illustrious history, but today the place is a little past its prime. It mainly features traditional French bands. Good for dancing and, if you're young, making contact. Stays open especially late on Fridays and Saturdays. Entrance 45–55 frs. Inexpensive drinks.

Le Montana, 28 rue St.-Benoît, 6e (tel. 45-48-93-08). An informal bar in the heart of Saint-Germain-des-Prés. It sometimes has live piano jazz.

New Morning, 7–9 rue des Petites Ecuries, 10e (tel. 45-23-51-41). A large room (seats over 400) with excellent sound and visibility. Although it's only been going since 1981, this is now the best club in Paris, if not in Europe, and the premier venue for visiting American musicians, top French groups, and fashionable *salsa* bands. A serious place, for aficionados only. Entrance prices range from 90–120 frs. Moderate range of cocktails, spirits, and beers.

Le Petit Journal, 71 blvd. St.-Michel, 5e (tel. 43-26-28-59). Well run and long established club, opposite the Luxembourg Gardens, specializing in live traditional and mainstream jazz. Individual booths, unusual cocktails, lavish salads and ice-creams. Entrance and first drink 65–75 frs., second drink 40 frs. Closed Sunday and August.

Le Petit Opportun, 15 rue des Lavandières-Sainte-Opportune, 1e (tel. 42-36-01-36). Converted bistro with cramped atmospheric basement (seats 50) often featuring top-flight American soloists with French rhythm sections. Entrance and first drink up to 100 frs. At street level there's a pleasant bar with recorded music and less expensive drinks.

Slow Club, 130 rue de Rivoli, 1e (tel. 42-33-84-30). Long-established dancing club often presenting Maxim Saury's well-known traditional band. Open especially late at weekends. Entrance 50–60 frs.; inexpensive drinks.

Le Sunset, 60 rue des Lombards, 1e (tel. 42-61-46-60). In the reinvigorated Les Halles area: a small whitewashed cellar with first-rate live music. Clientele is young, chic, and there to listen. Open very late, and stays crowded. Entrance, including first drink, about 70 frs., second drink 50 frs. Long list of cocktails.

ROCK. Unlike French jazz, French rock is generally not considered to be up to much. It has certainly never achieved an international reputation. You should be able to get to hear live rock music in the following places, most of which charge in the region of 80–100 frs. entrance money, including the first drink, and around 45–55 frs. for subsequent drinks. Prices often rise on weekends, when most places get pretty crowded. Most don't get going properly till 11:30 or midnight, and stay open through to dawn or thereabouts.

Les Bains, 7 rue du Bourg-l'Abée, 3 (tel. 48-87-01-80). See "Discos" in *Nightlife* chapter. Has live rock on Wednesday nights.

Bus Palladium, 6 rue Fontaine, 9e (tel. 48-74-54-99). On the edge of Montmartre, youthful clientele, mostly live rock, some discs.

Gibus, 18 rue fbg. du Temple, 10e (tel. 47-00-78-88). See "Discos" in *Nightlife* chapter. Currently *the* place for rock.

Le Palace, 8 rue du Faubourg-Montmarte, 9e (tel. 42-46-10-87). See "Discos" in *Nightlife* chapter. Has live rock at times.

Rose Bonbon, 34 rue de la Roquette, 11e (tel. 48-06-69-58). Near the Bastille in downmarket eastern Paris. Has live rock every night of the week.

CLASSICAL CONCERTS. Paris is one of Europe's liveliest cities for contemporary music these days. This is thanks partly to the influence of Pierre Boulez, France's greatest living composer-conductor, who heads the contemporary music section at the **Pompidou/Beaubourg Center.** Interesting concerts are given there most of the year. Classical concerts are often held in the city's concert halls and, perhaps more interestingly for foreign visitors, in her historic churches. This is a splendid way of combining the delights of sightseeing with listening to music. Have a look to see if there's a concert being performed in **Notre-Dame, Saint-Louis-des-Invalides, Saint-Germain-l'Auxerrois, Saint-Merri,** or the **Sainte Chapelle,** all of which provide stunning settings. The concerts in the marvelous Gothic Sainte Chapelle are out of this world, especially if you're lucky enough to hit a time when they're performed by candlelight. Leaflets covering six months of programs can be obtained from the Paris Tourist Office or the Sainte Chapelle itself, and you'd be well advised to reserve well ahead if possible.

In the summer, the excellent *Festival de l'Ile-de-France* stages fine concerts of classical music in churches, abbeys, châteaux, and town halls all over the Ile de France, the area immediately around Paris. This again gives you an opportunity to combine an evening's concert going with a spot of sightseeing. And during the *Festival du Marais* in Paris, concerts are often performed in the courtyards of the Marais's beautifully restored mansions.

MOVIES

Paris has hundreds of movie houses, some huge and palatial, some tiny and uncomfortable. Parisians are far more addicted to the cinema as an art form than Londoners or New Yorkers, and you'll find that the latest films, French or foreign, are widely discussed. The letters "v.f." (*version française*) beside a foreign film in a newspaper or magazine listing mean that the movie has been dubbed into French; the letters "v.o." (*version originale*) mean that the movie is playing in the original language with French subtitles.

The bigger and more expensive movie houses are mostly on the Champs Elysées or around the Opéra. The smaller art houses are in the Latin Quarter or Saint-Germain-des-Près. Programs change on Wednesdays. The standard program has movies showing at two-hourly intervals between around 2 P.M. and midnight (later on

Fridays and Saturdays). Prices are lower on Mondays except when it is a public holiday.

Paris has two *cinémathèques,* showing classics from all over the world, one in the Beaubourg/Pompidou Center, 4e, the other at the Palais de Chaillot in the Place du Trocadéro, 16e.

Theaters

NATIONAL THEATERS. The shows are naturally in French, so if your command of the language isn't great, you may find them heavy going. Paris's best-known "national" (i.e. state-subsidized) theaters are:

The **Comédie Française,** near the Opéra and beside the Palais-Royal in the place André-Malraux. The company specializes in performances of the great dramatists of the 17th century—Corneille, Molière, and Racine—but also ranges well beyond the classical repertoire, staging plays by modern playwrights from France and all over the world. Seats can be reserved in person a maximum of one week in advance.

The **Théâtre de Chaillot,** in the place du Trocadéro, has some interesting experimental shows from time to time.

The **Odéon,** in the place de l'Odéon in the Latin Quarter, is used mainly as an overspill for the Comédie Française, but also houses visiting companies, including major foreign troupes (such as Britain's Royal Shakespeare Company) playing in their own language.

The **Théâtre de la Ville** in the place du Châtelet stages a major international theater festival, plus opera and ballet at times.

COMMERCIAL THEATERS. For the many commercial theaters, most of which are in the Opéra area, you'll need to study lists of what's currently on. A surprising number of plays turn out to be translations of American or British hits, but you may find productions of movies by such well-known French dramatists as Jean Anouilh, Henri de

Montherlant, or the ever-green Ionesco. Many English-speaking visitors find French acting rather declamatory and strangely "theatrical."

EXPERIMENTAL THEATERS. You may well find that one of the experimental theaters is more to your taste. True theater buffs should check out what's showing at the following:

Cartoucherie, av. de la Pyramide, on the edge of Paris at Vincennes. Several resident companies here, with invariably interesting, sometimes way-out, shows. At our presstime these four separate mini-theaters were operating, but be sure to check the latest position: **Epée de Bois,** tel. 48-08-39-74; **Théâtre de la Tempête,** tel. 43-28-36-36; **Atelier du Chaudron,** tel. 43-28-97-04; **Théâtre de l'Aquarium,** tel. 43-74-99-61.

Epicerie, 12 rue du Renard, 3e, tel. 42-72-23-41, near Beaubourg and the Hôtel de Ville.

Lucernaire, 53 rue Notre-Dame-des-Champs, 6e, tel. 45-44-57-34, with two separate theaters, the **Théâtre Noir** and the **Théâtre Rouge,** each generally offering two different shows nightly.

Rond-Point, av. Franklin-Roosevelt, 8e, tel. 42-56-70-80; the **Petite Salle** in this very attractive former ice-skating palace, now housing the world-famous Madeleine Renaud–Jean-Louis Barrault company, often has interesting semi-experimental shows.

OPERA AND BALLET

Fortunately, you don't need a knowledge of French to enjoy the excellent productions at the **Paris Opéra,** the opulent building in the place de l'Opéra, generally considered to be one of the world's great houses. But you'll probably have a lot of trouble getting tickets.

The **Opéra Comique** (also known as the **Salle Fayart**) is Paris's second opera house. It specializes in opera with spoken dialogue (which is what the term *opéra comique* means).

The Opéra is also the home of the state-subsidized ballet company, which has a fairly high reputation. Much of the most interesting ballet in Paris comes during the annual November–December Ballet Festival held in the **Théâtre des Champs-Elysées** in the avenue Montaigne. Major foreign companies and guest stars perform during this excellent festival. Other places where ballet is staged are the **Théâtre de la Ville,** the huge **Palais des Congrès,** and the **Palais des Sports** at the Porte de Versailles. This last is not as atmospheric as the Opéra, but it is able to seat thousands of people. The huge **Théâtre Musical de Paris,** in the place du Châtelet, offers opera and ballet intended for a more popular audience, with much lower seat prices than at the Opéra. You may also find productions at the ultra-modern **Palais Omnisports de Bercy** in eastern Paris. A new "popular opera house" is currently being built at the Bastille and should open in 1989.

Keep an eye open for ballet performances during the *Festival du Marais* in the early summer, and the *Festival Estival* (Summer Festival), which runs from mid-July to around mid-September. Outside Paris, opera (and occasionally ballet) is staged in the pretty opera house in Versailles.

Shopping

We're ready to bet you'll find shopping in Paris one of the highlights of your trip. There's a huge range of shops, from the mammoth department stores to tiny back-street haunts selling a wide range of charming handmade gift items. And then there are the fabulous open-air markets, boasting everything from aardvarks to zebra fish, and almost always with prices lower than in regular shops.

Paris being a thoroughly cosmopolitan city, you can buy pretty much anything here. But so you can back home, too. So we've concentrated on the sorts of typically French goods you're likely to want to take back as souvenirs, or give to friends and family.

SHOPPING FACTS

Shops are open from 9 or 10 A.M. to 6:30 or 7 P.M. Fashion boutiques and antique shops may not open until 10 and may shut for lunch, especially in the summer when some staff are on vacation. Small food shops open earlier (8 or 8:30) and don't close until around 7:30 or 8 P.M., but they have a long lunch break, usually from 12:30 or 1 to 3:30 or 4. Department stores stay open all day, from around 9:30 to 6:30. Many small shops close for at least a month in the summer, when most of their regular customers are away from Paris, but a surprising number of shops are open on Sunday mornings, and small food shops are generally open in the morning on public holidays. However, Monday is a bad day for food shopping, as many food shops are closed in the morning. Many other shops that are open all day on Saturday may well close for at least part of Monday.

If you're resident outside France, you'll generally be able to take advantage of the tax-free refunds many stores offer. The best places to do so are the department stores and the larger fashion and perfume boutiques. A significant part of their business comes from tourists, and they have all the paperwork well organized. Other shops may do their best to be helpful, but the odds are they won't be equipped to deal efficiently with the formalities, and you may never get your refund. For details of how the scheme works, see "Tax Refunds" in *Paris Briefing*.

A good many larger stores will accept dollars or pounds—either travelers checks or bills—for goods. But their exchange rates often bear little more than a passing resemblance to the official one, and any gain in convenience may be paid for in hard cash, making this a mixed blessing. Credit cards are becoming more widely accepted, but by no means universally.

You can have goods sent directly to your home, but this is a chancy business at best. Goods have often been "lost" en route. Many stores, even the largest, are ever more reluctant to do this now, fearing for their reputations. But if you do have goods sent home, expect them to take many weeks, even if they go by air.

Department stores

The city has a large number of excellent department stores. **Au Printemps,** 64 blvd. Haussmann, 9e, claims to be the "most Parisian of the big stores." It is certainly one of the most upmarket, as is the long-famous **Galeries Lafayette,** next door at 40. These two huge stores have everything, including restaurants, hairdressers, and multilingual hostesses. Not far from here is the smaller and very select **Trois-Quartiers,** 17 blvd. de la Madeleine, 1er.

Two popular stores catering more to ordinary Parisians than to foreign tourists are close together in the Hôtel de Ville area: **La Samaritaine,** 19 rue de la Monnaie, 1er, with a roof terrace offering stunning views over the Seine; and the **Bazar de l'Hôtel de Ville,** 55 rue de le Verrerie, 4e (main entrances in the rue de Rivoli, just opposite the Hôtel de Ville), which is excellent for household articles.

The only department store on the Left Bank is **Au Bon Marché,** 38 rue de Sèvres, 7e, with a well-known antiques section, and a faithful following among local residents.

Shopping arcades and malls

The city's covered shopping arcades, many dating from the 19th century, are peculiarly Parisian. The best have been splendidly restored to show off to full advantage their arching glass roofs, marble floors, brass lamps, and, in one or two instances, even an elaborate staircase.

Two of the most attractive are the **Galerie Véro-Dodat,** 19 rue Jean-Jacques Rousseau, 1er, with magnificent painted ceilings and slender copper pillars, and the **Galerie Vivienne,** 4 pl. des Petits-Champs, 3e, near the

Bourse and the Bibliothèque Nationale, which has some particularly interesting shops, as well as a good tearoom. Other examples, all in the same central area of the Right Bank, are the **Passage des Pavillons,** 6 rue de Beaujolais, 1er; the **Passage des Princes,** 97 rue de Richelieu, 2e; and the **Passage des Panoramas,** 2e, the granddaddy of them all—it was opened to the public as long ago as 1800.

This 19th-century tradition has been revived in recent times with the building of several *galeries* off the Champs Elysées (all on the north side). The **Galerie du Claridge, Galeries Elysées 26, Galeries du Lido,** and **Galerie du Rond Point** are all worth seeking out. The **Forum des Halles** and the first floor of the **Tour Montparnasse** are larger versions still—more malls than arcades—though entirely lacking the architectural grace of the old arcades.

MARKETS

Paris's open-air **food markets** are an unending delight. The colorful pyramids of fruits and vegetables are particularly appealing, but don't touch the goods or you'll be treated to some equally colorful language from the stallholder!

Over Christmas and New Year the stallholders really go to town, vying with one another to produce the most tempting displays of seasonal specialties: fruits and nuts, every conceivable type of *charcuterie,* with *foie gras* and pâtés fashioned to look like miniature ducks, and terrines decorated with seasonal trimmings.

Every district has its own market, which may be held daily or just once or twice a week, though in all cases the morning is always the best time to visit. Sunday is usually the best day for market lovers, and Monday the worst. The best-known of the food markets are: the centuries-old rue Mouffetard, 5e, in the heart of the Latin Quarter; the rue de Buci and the rue de Seine, 6e, bang in the middle of St.-Germain-des-Prés; the rue Clerc, 7e, near the Invalides and the Eiffel Tower; the rue Poncelet, 17e, close to pl. des Ternes; the rue Lepic, 18e, in Montmartre; and the pl. du Marché in Neuilly (just by the Les Sablons métro stop), this last a good bet if you feel like a Sunday stroll in the Bois de Boulogne (though it's also open Wednesday and Friday).

The most famous **flower market** is on the Ile de la Cité, near Notre Dame, but there are equally good flower markets beside the church of La Madeleine, 8e, and in the pl. des Ternes, 17e. All are open daily except Monday from 8 to 7.

The most famous market of all is the Marché aux Puces, the **flea market,** founded in 1885. It's held around the Porte de St.-Ouen, 17e, and the Porte de St.-Clignancourt, 18e, and spreads over an astounding six-and-a-half kilometers. It's open all day Saturday, Sunday, and Monday, but get here early if you're after bargains.

Perfumes

What could be more French than a bottle of one of the world's top perfumes? But buying perfumes here can be a complicated business, especially if you want the best possible price. Everybody seems to be offering discounts of one kind or another, and the hard sell is very much the norm. But if you're prepared to take your time and shop around, and take advantage of the tax refunds, there are some great bargains.

If you already know what you want, head for one of the upmarket discount stores. Try **Liz** at 194 rue de Rivoli, 1er; **Galerie Elysées 26** at 26 av. des Champs-Elysées, 8e; and 112 rue du fbg. St.-Honoré, 8e; or the old-established **Michel Swiss,** 16 rue de la Paix, 2e. **Paris Look,** 13 av. de l'Opéra, 1er, advertises 25% off the major names; and **Patchouli,** at 3 and 50 rue du Cherche-Midi, 6e, which is also a beauty salon, offers 20% off. Two reliable family-run discount businesses are **Catherine,** 6 rue de Castiglione, 1er, and **Maréchal,** 232 rue de Rivoli, 1er. If what you know you want happens to be a **Guer-**

lain, you must head for one of their own exclusive boutiques, at 2 pl. Vendôme, 1er; 29 rue de Sèvres, 6e; 68 av des Champs-Elysées, 8e; or 93 rue de Passy, 16e.

If your main aim is to sniff a wide variety of perfumes, aim either for the **Galeries Lafayette** or **Printemps** near the Opéra, or **Sephora,** 50 rue de Passy, 16e, and the Forum des Halles. Sephora claims to be the world's largest perfumery store.

FASHION

If you can afford **haute couture**—and make no mistake, we're talking big bucks—sally forth to the av. Montaigne, 8e. Here you'll find such hardy perennials as **Christian Dior, Guy Laroche, Nina Ricci,** and **Emanuel Ungaro.** Alternatively, make your way to the rue au Faubourg St.-Honoré, 8e, for **Louis Feraud, Lanvin,** and **Torrente.** Most of the other big names are in streets adjoining one of these two: **Balmain, Courrèges** and **Ted Lapidus** in the rue François-1er; **Givenchy** in the av. George-V; **Yves Saint-Laurent** in the av. Marceau; **Chloé** in the av. Franklin-Roosevelt; **Chanel** in the rue Cambon.

St.-Germain-des-Prés is the place for more avant-garde styles. Try any of the following *couture* designers: **Sonia Rykiel,** 6 rue de Grenelle, and **Chantal Thomass,** 11 rue Madame, and many long-famous boutiques such as **Dorothée Bis,** 33 rue de Sèvres; **Anastasia,** 18 rue de l'Ancienne-Comédie; **Gudule,** 72 rue St.-André-des-Arts, and **Tiffany,** 12 rue de Sèvres. All of these specialize in ready-to-wear. You'll also find a wealth of attractive and up-to-the-minute fashions in the huge number of boutiques in and around the blvd. St.-Germain. **La Gaminerie,** 137 blvd. St.-Germain, is an old favorite, with good accessories too.

The place des Victoires, near the newly renovated Les Halles district, has become one of *the* centers of avant-garde fashion. Come here for the great **Kenzo,** and for good selections in **France Andrévie** and **Victoire.** In and around Les Halles itself **Agnès B,** in the rue du Jour, is a favorite with lovers of sophisticated yet wearable outfits, while the punningly named **Halles Capone,** 12 rue Turbigo, 1er, is very "in" for well-cut jeans.

Accessories

The rue Tronchet is a good place for accessories. **La Bagagerie** at 22 is a reliable store for beautiful bags and purses to go with your new outfit, while **Carel** at 4 has really fabulous shoes, as does **Renast** at 33. **Hélion,** at 22, specializes in sleek gloves. The city's most famous sellers of leather goods are all in this part of Paris, with the great **Hermès** a short walk away in the fbg. St.-Honoré, at 24, and two major specialists at 265 and 271 rue St.-Honoré: **Sellerie de la Cour** and **Sellerie de France. Lancel,** in the place de l'Opéra, is another good bet.

On the Left Bank, **La Bagagerie** has another store in the rue de Rennes, while several good shoe shops are nearby: **Carel** and **Tilbury** in the rue du Four, **Cassandre, Céline,** and **Charles Jourdan** in the rue de Rennes, **François Villon** at 58 rue Bonaparte, and trendy **Maud Frizon** at 83 rue des Sts.-Pères.

Most of the city's fashion boutiques sell some accessories carefully selected to go with their outfits, and you should also consider examining the huge range of bags and purses, silk headscarves, and fashionable umbrellas in the department stores. Some of the open-air markets have bargains in shoes and bags, too. And talking of bargains, you may like to know about the **Club des 10,** 58 rue du fbg. St.-Honoré, 8e, which offers 30–40% off designs by some of the best-known *couture* and ready-to-wear names.

EDIBLE GOODIES

Pretty boxes of French regional specialties can be found in many places in Paris, from the little corner grocery or bakery to the gastronomic temples, such as those two *very* superior grocers, **Fauchon,** at 26 pl. de la Madeleine, 8e, or **Hédiard,** also in the pl. de la Madeleine, at 21, and at 126 rue du Bac, 7e, 106 blvd. de Courcelles, 17e, and in the Forum des Halles.

Those with a sweet tooth will be tempted by the *fruits confits* (candied fruit) of southern France, or by local specialties such as *calissons d'Aix* or *bergamotes de Nancy*, as well as many other types of sweets or candies. Delicious nougat from Montmélimar comes in all shapes, sizes, and colors. Beautifully arranged boxes of wrapped hard candy are a delight to the eye as well as the palate, while perhaps nicest of all, and very typically French, are the delightful yet inexpensive little boxes or oval tins of *réglisse* (licorice), whose presentation hasn't changed for centuries. **Aux Douceurs de France,** 70 blvd. de Strasbourg, 10e, specializes in candies from all over France, but you'll find many of them in other food shops.

For great French chocolates try **Ballotin,** 41 rue Montorgueil, 2e, close to Les Halles.

Tins or cans of *foie gras*, or truffles, will delight a gourmet's heart. Snails and preserved wild mushrooms in cans or glass jars are other delicacies you won't find easily back home.

As for wine, corner groceries or the **Nicolas** chain of wine shops will suit your picnic needs, and will provide bottles to take home if you prefer not to use the duty-free shops at the airports. But if you want something really special, don't miss **Vins Rares et de Collection,** 3 rue Laugier, 17e, which has a large selection of France's most famous vintages.

If you do plan to take home any food products, remember that you may not import into the US any fresh meats, fruits, plants, or other agricultural products.

Gorgeous gifts

For those who want to find a more unusual gift we've picked out a few places that have something really special on offer.

For instance, **Isabelle Valogne,** 53 av. de la Bourdonnais, 7e, specializes in charming scent bottles, both antique and modern, and also has some fine Art Deco brooches. **La Rose des Vents,** 65 rue de Seine, 6e, is a pretty little shop with a good range of "natural products" —pots pourris, scented soaps, dried flowers, natural beauty products, candles, and the like. **Monsieur Renard,** 6 rue de l'Echaudé, 6e, is full of antique dolls and automata. **Le Monde en Marche,** 34 rue Dauphine, 6e, with many wooden toys and puppets, is a good place for presents for small children. **Françoise Thibault,** 1 rue Jacob, 6e, and 1 rue Bourbon-le-Château, 6e, is an old favorite for attractive gifts, with some delightful handpainted boxes and picture frames. **Léon,** 220 rue de Rivoli, 1er, has been going for over 100 years, and is a must for magical little porcelain boxes decorated with flowers, exquisite thimbles, and paperweights, as well as reproductions of Sèvres porcelain.

If you prefer to take home an antique object, try the **Louvre des Antiquaires** emporium in the pl. du Palais-Royal, 1er, the **Village Suisse,** 52 av. de la Motte-Piquet, 15e, the **Cour des Saints-Pères,** off the street of the same name, 7e, or the **Jardins Saint-Paul,** again off the street of the same name, which also has some craft stalls and workshops.

And for art-lovers a print makes a good buy. The best area to try is the rue de Seine, 6e, and the surrounding streets, including the bookstalls along by the river. On the Right Bank, the happiest hunting ground is the avenue Matignon, 8e, but prices here are high. The **Department Chalcographique** in the Louvre, containing thousands of prints from old plates, is another must if you've set your heart on a print.

Index

Abbaye Saint-Germain, L'*(hotel)*, 68
Absinthe, L' *(rest.)*, 74
A Priori-Thé (tea shop), 32
Afruitisiaque, L'(ice cream & fruit bar), 48
  information, 89
Airport transportation, 5–6
Alsace *(rest.)*, 82
Amanguier, L', *(rest.)*, 76
Ambassade d' Auvergne *(rest.)*, 77
Angleterre *(hotel)*, 68
Apartment rentals, 65
Arc de Triomphe, 21
Arc de Triomphe du Carrousel, 24
Atelier Maître Albert *(rest.)*, 79
August closings, 16
Au Quai d'Orsay *(rest.)*, 82
Aux Charpentiers *(rest.)*, 80
Avenir *(hotel)*, 67
Avenue de l'Opéra, 36–37
Avenue d'Iéna, 19
Avenue Georges V, 22

Balzar, Le *(rest.)*, 79
Bar du Caveau *(rest.)*, 53
Bars, 87–88
B.D. 36 *(rest.)*, 80
Beaubourg Center, 43, 44–45
  concerts in, 97
  information, 45
Berthillon (ice cream shop), 49
Bibliothèque Nationale, 32
Bicycle rentals, 10

Bistro de la Gare *(rest.)*, 74
Bistro du Fort, *(rest.)*, 33
  information, 76
Bistrot Vivienne, 31
Boat trips, 7, 10
Bonaparte (café), 59
Boulevard de Clichy, 41
Boulevard des Capucines, 34
Boulevard des Italiens, 33
Boulevard de Sébastopol, 43–44
Boulevard du Montparnasse, 58–59
Boulevard Haussmann, 36
Boulevard Montmarte, 33
Boulevard St-Germain, 54, 59
Boulevard St-Michel, 54, 55
Bourse, the, 32
Brasserie de l'Ile St-Louis, 49
Bretonnerie *(hotel)*, 67
Bristol *(hotel)*, 70
Bus tours, 7
Bus transportation, 7

Cabécou, Le *(rest.)*, 80
Cafe de la Paix, 85
Cafés, 85–86
  information, 85
Casa Miguel *(rest.)*, 83
Centre National d'Art et de Culture Georges Pompidou. *See* Beaubourg Center
Chambiges *(hotel)*, 70
Champs Elysées, 21–23
Chez des Anges *(rest.)*, 81
Chez Françoise *(rest.)*, 81–82

113

INDEX

Chez Paul (*rest.*), 53
Chez Pauline (*rest.*), 75
Chez Philippe (*rest.*), 84
Choiseul-Opéra (*hotel*), 66
Church of St. Roch, 36
Classiques, Les (*rest.*), 80
Climate, 3–4
Closerie des Lilas (*rest/bar*), 59
  information, 87
Clothing, 4
Clubs, 92–93
Colbert (*hotel*), 67–68
Colombe, La (*rest.*), 78
Comédie Francaise, 31
  information, 99
Conciergerie, The, 52–53
Coupole, La (*café/brasserie*), 59
  information, 85–86
Courrier Sud (*rest.*), 78
Crazy Horse Saloon, 22
  information, 91
Credit cards, 3
Crillon (*hotel*), 70
Currency & exchange, 3
Currency regulations, 5
Customs regulations, 5

Daniel Tuboeuf (*rest.*), 77
Delacroix (studio of), 60
Department stores & shops, 36.
  See also Shopping
Deux-Iles (*hotel*), 67
Deux Magots, Aux (*café*), 59
  information, 86
Discos, 93–94
Discounts. *See* Tax refunds
Dodin Bouffant (*rest.*), 79
Domarais, Le (*rest.*), 78
Dôme, Le (*café/brasserie*), 59
  information, 86
Duty-free allowance, 4–5

Edouard-VII (*hotel*), 66

Eiffel Tower, 18–19
  (*rest./bar*), 19
English language information, 2
Escargot Montorgueil, L' (*rest.*), 74
Esmeralda (*hotel*), 68

Family Hotel, 65
Flamel, Nicholas (house of & restaurant), 44
Flore, Le (*café*), 59
  information, 86
Folies Bergère, 41
  information, 91
Fontaine de Mars, La (*rest.*), 81
Food products (U.S.A. import restrictions), 109
Forum (shopping complex), 43–44
Fouquet's (*café*), 86
French National Tourist Office
  in Britain, 1
  in Paris, 1–2
  in U.S.A. & Canada, 1

Galérie Colbert, 31–32
Galérie Vivienne, 31–32
George V (*hotel*), 70
Gérard Besson (*rest.*), 74
Gourmet's (*rest.*), 74
Grandes Ecoles (*hotel*), 68
Grand Palais, 22
Grands Boulevards, 36–37
Grand Véfour (*rest.*), 31
  information, 74–75

Harry's Bar, 87
Helicopter tours, 10
Hippoptamus, L' (*rest.*), 22
History & background of Paris, 14–16
Holy Trinity Church, 22
Hôtel de Rohan, 45–46

INDEX

Hôtel de Soubise, 45–46
Hôtel de Ville, 48
  information, 48
Hotel, L', 68
Hotels, 64–71
  information, 64–65
  1st Arrondissement, 65–66
  2nd Arrondissement, 66
  3rd Arrondissement, 66–67
  4th Arrondissement, 67
  5th Arrondissement, 67–68
  6th Arrondissement, 68–69
  7th Arrondissement, 69–70
  8th Arrondissement, 70–71

Ile de la Cité, 50–53
Ile St-Louis, 49–50
Information sources, 1–3. See also alphabetical listings
Introduction to Paris, 12–17

Janou (*rest.*), 77
Jardin des Plantes, 55
Jardin du Luxembourg, 55
Jaurès, 42
Jeu de Paume, 23, 24
Jewish quarter, 48
Juice bars, 89
Jules Verne (*rest.*), 19
  information, 82

La Madeleine, 34–35
Lancaster (*hotel*), 71
Lapin Agile, Le (*café*), 41
  information, 91–92
La Rose Daisy (*rest.*), 48
  information, 78
Latin Quarter, 54
Left Bank, 54–63

Les Champs (shopping center), 21
Lido (*nightclub*), 92
Limousine tours, 7
Lipp (*café*), 59
  information, 86
Londres Stockholm (*hotel*), 65
Louisiane, La (*hotel*), 68–69
Louvre, The, 25–28
  Apollo Gallery, 26
  Cour Carré, 25
  Glass Pyramid, 26
  Grande Gallery, 26
  information, 27–28
  Mona Lisa, 26–27
  Salle Daru, 27
  Salle Mollien, 27
  Salon Carré, 26
Lucas-Carton-Alain Senderens (*rest.*), 82–83
Lutèce (*hotel*), 67
Lutétia (*hotel*), 69
Luxembourg Palace, 55, 58

Ma Bourgogne (*rest.*), 47
Madeleine. *See* La Madeleine
Maison Blanche, La (*rest.*), 84
Maps
  arrondissements, 13
  Champs Elysées, 20
  Ile de la Cité, 50
  Left Bank, 56–57
  Louvre, The, 28
  Marais, 46
  Métro, 8–9
  Montmartre, 39
  Opéra area, 30
  Paris, viii–ix
Marais (*hotel*), 66–67
Marais, The, 45–48
Marigny (theaters), 22
Maxim's (*rest.*), 83
Mercure Galant (*rest.*), 75
Métro, 6–7

INDEX

Milles Feuilles, Le (*rest.*), 77
Mitidja Oriental (*rest.*), 33
Modern Art Museum (Beaubourg Center), 45
Montmartre, 38–42
　cabarets & nightlife, 41
Montmartre Cemetery, 40
Montparnasse, 58–59
Moulin Rouge, 41
　information, 92
Movies, 98–99
Musée Carnavalet, 47
Musée Cognac Jay, 34
Musée d'Art Juif, 40
Musée d'Art Moderne de la Ville de Paris, 19–20
Musée de Cluny, 54–55
　information, 55
Musée de la Chasse, 47
Musée de L'Armée, 63
Musée de Montmartre, 41
Musée d'Orsay, 61–62
　(*café & rest. in*), 62
Musée Edith Piaf, 42
Musée Grevin, 33
Musée Guimet, 19
Musée Gustav Moreau, 41–42
Musée Picasso, 47
Musée Rodin, 62
Musée Victor Hugo, 47
Museums & galleries, 19–23, 24–28, 33, 34, 35, 40, 41, 42, 45–46, 47, 54–55, 60, 61–62, 63. *See also* alphabetical listings & *under* musée
Music, 95–98
　classical concerts, 97–98
　jazz, 95–97
　rock, 97

National Library, The. *See* Bibliothèque Nationale
Newspapers & magazines, 2

Nightlife, 90–95
　information, 90. (*See also* alphabetical listings)
Noailles, Le (*rest.*), 75
Normandy, (*hotel*), 65
Notre Dame, 51–52
　concerts at, 98

Obelisk of Luxor, 23
Opera and ballet, 100–101
Opéra Comique. *See* Salle Fayart
Opera d'Antin l'Horset (*hotel*), 66
Opéra House. *See* Paris Opéra House
Orangerie, 23, 24–25

Palais (*hotel*), 65
Palais de Chaillot, 19
　museums in, 19
Palais de Justice, 52
Palais de Tokyo, 19–20
Palais Garnier. *See* Paris Opera House
Palais Royale, 29–31
Panthéon, 55
Parc des Buttes Chaumonts, 42
Paris Observatory, 58
Paris Opéra & House of, 33–34
　information, 100
Passage des Deux Pavillons, 31
Passage des Panoramas, 33
Passports, 4
Patisserie shops (Ile St-Louis), 49
Pavillon du Lac (*rest.*), 42
Perraudin (*rest.*), 79
Petit Coin de la Bourse, Le (*rest.*), 76
Petite Chaise, La (*rest.*), 82
Petit Palais, 22

INDEX 117

Petit St-Benoit (*rest.*), 80–81
Petit Zinc, Le (*rest.*), 81
Pharamond (*rest.*), 75
Pierre à la Fontaine Gaillon (*rest.*), 76
Pile ou Face (*rest.*), 77
Place de la Concorde, 22–23
Place de l'Hôtel de Ville, 48
Place de l'Opèra, 33
Place des Victories, 31
Place des Vosges, 47
Place du 18 Juin, 1940, 58
Place du Terte, 41
Place Furstemberg, 60
Place Vendôme, 35–36
Point Show (shopping center), 21
Pont Alexandre III, 22
Pont-Royal (*hotel*), 69
Pont St-Louis, 50
Procope, Le (*rest.*), 80
Pullman, Le (*rest.*), 31
Pyramid, 24, 26

Quai des Ormes (*rest.*), 78

Résidence Elysées-Maubourg (*hotel*), 69
Restaurant des Saints-Péres, 81
Restaurants, 72–84
  information, 72–73
  lst Arrondissement, 74–76
  2nd Arrondissement, 76–77
  3rd Arrondissement, 77
  4th Arrondissement, 78
  5th Arrondissement, 79–80
  6th Arrondissement, 80–81
  7th Arrondissement, 81–82
  8th Arrondissement, 82–83
  9th Arrondissement, 83
  11th Arrondissement, 84
  15th Arrondissement, 84
  17th Arrondissement, 84
Ritz (*hotel*), 65–66
Roblin (*hotel*), 71
Rond Point, 22
Rôtisserie-Rivoli (*rest.*), 75
Rue Bonaparte, 59
Rue de Beaujolais, 31
Rue de la Gaîté, 58
Rue de Rivoli, 37, 48
Rue des Collones, 32
Rue des Petits Champs, 31
Rue des Rosiers, 48
Rue de Seine, 59
Rue des Saules, 40–41
Rue du Faubourg-St-Honoré, 35, 36
Rue Montmorency, 44
Rue Rambuteau, 45

Sacré-Couer, 38, 40
Sainte-Chapelle, 52
  concerts at, 98
Saint-Louis (*hotel*), 67
Saints-Péres (*hotel*), 69
St-Germain, 59–60
St-Germain des-Prés, 59
St. Louis des Invalides, 63
St Louis en-l'Ile (church & street), 49
St-Martin canal, 42
St-Sulpice, 59
St-Vincent Cemetery, 40
Salle Favart, 33
  information, 100–101
Salon du Thé St-Louis, 49
Select, Le (*café*), 86
Shopping, 36, 102–110
  information, 102–103
  accessories, 108
  antiques, 110
  art, 110
  candies & sweets, 109
  department stores, 104
  fashion, 107–108

flea market, 106
flower market, 106
food market, 105–106
gifts, 110
grocers, 109
markets, 105–106
perfumes, 106–107
shopping arcades/malls, 104–105
wine, 109
Shows, 91–92
Sorbonne, The, 55
Stravinsky Fountain, 44
Subways. *See* Métro

Taillevent (*rest.*), 83
Taxis, 7
Tax refunds, 10–11
Theaters, 99–100
commercial theaters, 99–100
experimental theaters, 100
national theaters, 99
Théâtre de Champs Elysées, 22, 101
Time (local), 4
Tipping, 5

Tomb of the Unknown Soldier, 21
Toque, La (*rest.*), 84
Tour d'Argent, La (*rest.*), 79–80
Tour Maine-Montparnasse, 58
Tours, 7, 10
Transportation, 5–7, 10. *See also* alphabetical listings
Trattoria Toscana, 33
Traveler's checks, 3
Tremoille, Le (*hotel*), 71
Tuileries Gardens, 23, 26

Varenne (*hotel*), 70
Verneuil St.-Germain (*hotel*), 70
Vieux Paris (*hotel*), 69
Vilette St-Paul (*snack bar*), 48
Visas, 4

Westminster (*hotel*), 66
Willi's Wine Bar (*rest.*), 75–76
Wine bars, 88–89
information, 88

FODOR'S TRAVEL GUIDES

Here is a complete list of Fodor's Travel Guides, available in current editions; most are also available in a British edition published by Hodder & Stoughton.

U.S. GUIDES

Alaska
American Cities (Great Travel Values)
Arizona including the Grand Canyon
Atlantic City & the New Jersey Shore
Boston
California
Cape Cod & the Islands of Martha's Vineyard & Nantucket
Carolinas & the Georgia Coast
Chesapeake
Chicago
Colorado
Dallas/Fort Worth
Disney World & the Orlando Area (Fun in)
Far West
Florida
Fort Worth (see Dallas)
Galveston (see Houston)
Georgia (see Carolinas)
Grand Canyon (see Arizona)
Greater Miami & the Gold Coast
Hawaii
Hawaii (Great Travel Values)
Houston & Galveston
I-10: California to Florida
I-55: Chicago to New Orleans
I-75: Michigan to Florida
I-80: San Francisco to New York
I-95: Maine to Miami
Jamestown (see Williamsburg)
Las Vegas including Reno & Lake Tahoe (Fun in)
Los Angeles & Nearby Attractions
Martha's Vineyard (see Cape Cod)
Maui (Fun in)
Nantucket (see Cape Cod)
New England
New Jersey (see Atlantic City)
New Mexico
New Orleans
New Orleans (Fun in)
New York City
New York City (Fun in)
New York State
Orlando (see Disney World)
Pacific North Coast
Philadelphia
Reno (see Las Vegas)
Rockies
San Diego & Nearby Attractions
San Francisco (Fun in)
San Francisco plus Marin County & the Wine Country
The South
Texas
U.S.A.
Virgin Islands (U.S. & British)
Virginia
Waikiki (Fun in)
Washington, D.C.
Williamsburg, Jamestown & Yorktown

FOREIGN GUIDES

Acapulco (see Mexico City)
Acapulco (Fun in)
Amsterdam
Australia, New Zealand & the South Pacific
Austria
The Bahamas
The Bahamas (Fun in)
Barbados (Fun in)
Beijing, Guangzhou & Shanghai
Belgium & Luxembourg
Bermuda
Brazil
Britain (Great Travel Values)
Canada
Canada (Great Travel Values)
Canada's Maritime Provinces plus Newfoundland & Labrador
Cancún, Cozumel, Mérida & the Yucatán
Caribbean
Caribbean (Great Travel Values)
Central America
Copenhagen (see Stockholm)
Cozumel (see Cancún)
Eastern Europe
Egypt
Europe
Europe (Budget)
France
France (Great Travel Values)
Germany: East & West
Germany (Great Travel Values)
Great Britain
Greece
Guangzhou (see Beijing)
Helsinki (see Stockholm)
Holland
Hong Kong & Macau
Hungary
India, Nepal & Sri Lanka
Ireland
Israel
Italy
Italy (Great Travel Values)
Jamaica (Fun in)
Japan
Japan (Great Travel Values)
Jordan & the Holy Land
Kenya
Korea
Labrador (see Canada's Maritime Provinces)
Lisbon
Loire Valley
London
London (Fun in)
London (Great Travel Values)
Luxembourg (see Belgium)
Macau (see Hong Kong)
Madrid
Mazatlan (see Mexico's Baja)
Mexico
Mexico (Great Travel Values)
Mexico City & Acapulco
Mexico's Baja & Puerto Vallarta, Mazatlan, Manzanillo, Copper Canyon
Montreal (Fun in)
Munich
Nepal (see India)
New Zealand
Newfoundland (see Canada's Maritime Provinces)
1936... on the Continent
North Africa
Oslo (see Stockholm)
Paris
Paris (Fun in)
People's Republic of China
Portugal
Province of Quebec
Puerto Vallarta (see Mexico's Baja)
Reykjavik (see Stockholm)
Rio (Fun in)
The Riviera (Fun on)
Rome
St. Martin/St. Maarten (Fun in)
Scandinavia
Scotland
Shanghai (see Beijing)
Singapore
South America
South Pacific
Southeast Asia
Soviet Union
Spain
Spain (Great Travel Values)
Sri Lanka (see India)
Stockholm, Copenhagen, Oslo, Helsinki & Reykjavik
Sweden
Switzerland
Sydney
Tokyo
Toronto
Turkey
Vienna
Yucatán (see Cancún)
Yugoslavia

SPECIAL-INTEREST GUIDES

Bed & Breakfast Guide: North America
Royalty Watching
Selected Hotels of Europe
Selected Resorts and Hotels of the U.S.
Ski Resorts of North America
Views to Dine by around the World

AVAILABLE AT YOUR LOCAL BOOKSTORE OR WRITE TO FODOR'S TRAVEL PUBLICATIONS, INC., 201 EAST 50th STREET, NEW YORK, NY 10022.